"The most important event in my life occurred before I was born," one child of concentration camp survivors has observed. The Holocaust did not end with the liberation of survivors after the collapse of the Third Reich, for the legacy of their suffering extends to a generation that never faced an SS storm trooper. With a rich blend of oral history, memoir, and psychological interpretation, Aaron Hass deepens our understanding of the price of that legacy for the second generation.

What are the effects of growing up in the shadow of the Holocaust? Drawing on interviews and survey materials, Hass provides a vibrant account of the experiences of survivors' children. Now in their thirties and forties, these men and women describe their relationships with their parents and offer their perceptions of the impact of the Holocaust on their families. They give voice to memories and feelings about which some of them have never before spoken. Himself a child of survivors and a distinguished clinical psychologist, Hass writes about the lingering presence of the Holocaust in his own life as well.

In the Shadow of the Holocaust is an intimate account of how the survivors' responses to brutality and deprivation affected their later functioning as wives, husbands, and parents. Hass demonstrates that the range of responses is vast: from the survivor who hid his Jewish identity for fear of persecution and enrolled his child in Catholic parochial schools to the survivor who wore his Auschwitz uniform while conducting the Passover seder. In addition to frequently shared problems including depression, anger, guilt, feelings of being different, and difficulty in separating from parents, the interviews excerpted here reveal a remarkable diversity in the significance of the Holocaust in the lives of the second generation.

In the Shadow
of the Holocaust

In the Shadow
of the Holocaust

The Second Generation

AARON HASS

CAMBRIDGE
UNIVERSITY PRESS

Published by the Press Syndicate of the University of Cambridge
The Pitt Building, Trumpington Street, Cambridge CB2 1RP
40 West 20th Street, New York, NY 10011-4211, USA
10 Stamford Road, Oakleigh, Melbourne 3166, Australia

© Aaron Hass 1990

First published by Cornell University Press 1990

First Cambridge University Press edition 1996

Printed in the United States of America

Library of Congress Cataloging-in-Publication Data applied for.

A catalog record for this book is available from the British Library.

ISBN 0-521-58947-9 hardback
     0-521-49893-7 paperback

For Rachel and Sarah,
the third generation

Contents

Acknowledgments

I am grateful to Faber and Faber Ltd. for permission to reprint "Shema," from *Collected Poems* by Primo Levi, translated by Ruth Feldman and Brian Swann. I would like to express my appreciation to Michael Nutkiewicz and Florabel Kinsler for their sensitivity and kindness over the years. My gratitude to the children of survivors who shared with me their thoughts and experiences. My thanks to my wife, Rebecca, for her forbearance during the difficult times of this project. Finally, an author could not ask for a more enthusiastic and talented editor than Holly Bailey.

A. H.

Introduction

I have two recurring nightmares. In one, I move within a ghetto from hiding place to hiding place while attempting to elude Nazis. After a chase, I am captured, marched out of the ghetto, and with thousands of others herded onto a train, its destination a concentration camp. We travel for days. People moaning, fighting among themselves, crying, sick, forced to live in their own feces. We finally arrive at the station platform, where we are pushed and clubbed out of the cattle car and marched single file to a waiting gas chamber. In the other dream, I am in the Israeli army. The battle with the Arabs is fierce, the tide slowly turning against us. Our position, in a foxhole at the perimeter of a kibbutz in the desert or in a building in Tel Aviv, is overrun, and we are about to be slaughtered.

I am a forty-one-year-old clinical psychologist, university professor, husband, and father. But I am foremost a child of an earlier era. Events that occurred fifty years ago, before my birth, follow me. Stories of those times, images before my eyes, evoke my most intense feelings of anger, fear, and sadness. My parents, survivors of the Holocaust, raised me and shaped me.

Growing up meant being constrained, often paralyzed, by hearing, "How could you do this to me after all I have suffered?" My people—the Jews—and their history were, I felt, completely defined by suffering and oppression. In reaction, I formed attitudes about Gentiles, all Gentiles.

I have never been a joiner of groups. No Boy Scouts, no fraternities. I never belonged to a *group* of friends. I thought I was different from other children, and perhaps that self-perception resulted in my being seen by others as peculiar. I identified myself so narrowly. I was a remnant of the Holocaust. And, in a perverse manner, I believe I somewhat enjoyed this distinction, this uniqueness. As an adult, I continue to feel different from my contemporaries. Perhaps some of these feelings are simply a result of my temperament, a genetic legacy. But much of it I attribute to being a child of Holocaust survivors.

When asked, "Fin vanit bist du? (where are you from?)" by someone from the old country, I would respond "Ich bin a Lubliner." Even though before 1987 I had never been to Lublin, Poland, where my parents and grandparents lived before the war, I *felt* as though that were my home. Through a series of circumstances beyond my control, my life was displaced from where it should have taken place, from where, I believed, I would have led a far more contented existence.

I grew up thinking that laughing indicated a certain superficiality. It was not until I reached my thirties that I understood the value and necessity of laughter. I also had to learn not to begrudge it to others. I have similar, unusually strong, feelings about trivial conversation. I have no patience for it. I avoid it, and I know this inflexibility, this subversion of social etiquette, has cost me dearly, for it is usually perceived as snobbishness.

Since childhood I have been interested in the Holocaust—reading books, attending lectures, viewing films, inquiring about the past experiences of survivors—but only in recent years have I attempted to make sense of its impact on me and others close to me and to engage in activities such as teaching and writing that create hope and clarity as opposed to overwhelming sadness and opaqueness. Understanding the Holocaust's causes and its myriad effects after liberation has given me a greater sense of control over my life. I can now choose vehicles for personal expression and can place that era and its consequences in a useful, as opposed to simply painful, perspective. This book reflects a further attempt at comprehension. I embarked on the research for it without prior hypotheses. I was interested in discovering the extent to which other children of survivors had experiences similar to my own. I wanted to know if there were attitudes and patterns shared by those who had grown up in the shadow of the Holocaust.

In my reading, I found that much of the earlier research on children of Holocaust survivors, particularly that conducted in the 1970s, was deeply flawed by its focus on small, clinical samples, those children of survivors who were patients being seen in a psychiatric setting. It would be fallacious to assume these individuals were representative of the entire group. For convenience, other investigators have chosen subjects who were actively involved in organizations or activities of children of Holocaust survivors. But here, too, such a selection cannot be representative, since only a tiny percentage of children of survivors choose to affiliate or involve themselves in Holocaust-identified forums. In an attempt to increase the objectivity of their studies and produce quantifiable results, recent investigators have often used personality tests in their examination of children of survivors. As valid measures of personal qualities, unfortunately, such tests are often questionable and, more important, provide a constricted picture of the individual.

My own study was much less formal. It was based on personal interviews and a questionnaire and did not include a control group. I believe, however, that for the most part it avoided the pitfalls of the earlier studies.

Some of the participants were individuals I had met over the years. They provided the names and addresses of many friends and relatives who were also children of survivors. I requested face-to-face interviews with those in my geographical area and sent the questionnaire with an introduction and explanation for its rationale to those in distant locations. I introduced myself to potential participants as a professor of psychology and a child of survivors who was writing a book about children of survivors. I asked for their cooperation so that both laypeople and mental-health professionals could more fully understand the effects of growing up with such a background. (To preserve the anonymity of my informants, I have altered names and some characteristics. Some quotations are composites.)

It is difficult to obtain volunteers who are willing to commit several hours of their time for anything, let alone a process that may be distressing. Many to whom I sent the questionnaire never responded. Forty-eight children of Holocaust survivors agreed to be interviewed by me or responded anonymously to my questionnaire, forty-four from the United States and four from Canada. Each of the forty-eight had at least one parent who was in Nazi-occupied territory during World War II. They spanned the ages of nineteen to forty-two; two-thirds were between thirty and forty. Twenty-six occupations were represented, including teaching, the law, homemaking, medicine, selling, acting, and psychotherapy. A few of the respondents belonged to organizations of individuals from Holocaust backgrounds such as their own, but most did not. I conducted the interviews in 1988 over a period of one year, either in the subjects' homes or after hours in their offices.

While the items on my questionnaire were the same as those discussed in the personal interviews, I was able to follow up my queries during the face-to-face exchanges. In addition, I ended the interviews by asking: "Is there anything else about you and the Holocaust which you believe is important that I have failed to touch upon?" It became clear that many had never pieced together the relationship between various aspects of their personality and the Holocaust. I wished I had had more time with each subject. A lengthier interview might have fostered more insight and recognition.

Although my queries were specific, they encompassed concerns of my own that I believed were central issues in the life of a child of survivors. I hoped that my questions about parents would provide both information about the interaction between survivors and their children and a view of the survivors other than the one we have received from the survivors themselves or from mental-health professionals. In addition, I addressed a number of issues on which earlier research had not reported: belief in God, attitudes about Gentiles and about Israel, and views on the possibility of a recurrence of the Holocaust.

The questions I asked often required a consideration of issues that some preferred to leave unexamined. At the conclusion of our three hours together, one man commented that the conversation "was unsettling for me because I just haven't thought about how the Holocaust has affected these aspects of my life."

I encountered various levels of denial. When I asked one man why he avoided involvement in any Holocaust-related activities, he expressed the feelings of many survivor offspring who do not wish to be reminded of those events by their parents or by anything else: "Once I got the message, I didn't want to hear about it anymore. I know enough. The images are already indelible. To involve myself further would make me uncomfortable." Several people acknowledged that "it is just too painful for me to think about these things." One woman stated flatly, "The Holocaust happened to my parents. It has nothing to do with me."

Why did others agree to participate? Some were curious: "What do you think is important about my being a child of survivors? Are we different in some way?" Some were suspicious or insecure: "Are you looking for something?" or, with forced levity, "So, you want to see if we're screwed up."

Others, like Benjamin, were searching for answers about themselves and their families. We sat in his office at a large medical center late into the evening, and five times in the course of an emotional three-hour meeting, Benjamin, himself a physician, interjected, "You're going to have to send me a bill. What do you charge for sessions like this?"

Benjamin had moved three thousand miles away from his parents. Intense, nervous, and now thirty-six and a practicing neurosurgeon he had purposefully avoided contact with survivors or their children. He didn't want to think about that world. "Only negative things," he said, "can come from dwelling on the Holocaust." Yet he wondered. And when I called to ask for an interview, Benjamin was in the throes of marital difficulties. This was his second marriage. Neither wife was Jewish. It was a propitious time for him to take a look at himself.

Alex, a forty-year-old schoolteacher, lived with his wife and two children in a modest home in a middle-class suburb. Warm, articulate, and insightful, he had struggled to attain his stable, productive life. He had become a drug addict during his twenties, and the habit held him for ten years. His question to me, asked in various forms, reflected his agenda for our meeting. "Am I like other children of survivors?" If Alex was similar to other children of survivors, he could feel normal. His background could explain or justify his problems.

Before I began an interview, I expressed my appreciation to the person, usually a stranger, for his or her willingness to discuss personal issues with me. I expected that it might not be easy to talk about these things. Esther, a cheerful thirty-two-year-old Orthodox Jew who taught school, was quick to reassure me. "But you don't understand. This is a catharsis for me. I've looked forward to it ever since you called." Indeed, most children of survivors never have occasion to speak of their Holocaust background.

Some children of survivors were not at all reticent about speaking with me. Even during our initial telephone conversation it was clear that they were not simply interested in exposing *themselves* to me. "The world should know about us and what we went through," one man contended proudly. "I think we're a unique group. Our parents in particular. They're the real heroes."

Other children of survivors immediately agreed to participate for altruistic reasons. They were contributing to research in an area they believed was important—the Holocaust. "We must write about the Holocaust. It bothers me that they teach that the Holocaust never occurred. It's our duty to keep history alive," remarked one Israeli-born child of survivors. But even with these individuals, I invariably sensed other motivations as well. An opportunity to look inward. An opportunity to sort out who they were and where they came from. As one man explained, "For the first time I wanted to talk about it, see if I could gain some insight and find out if I could handle examining this stuff." The diversity of motives of these children of survivors was the first indication of the tremendous variety of responses they would report, both toward the Holocaust and toward their parents.

For myself, talking with other children of survivors was revelatory. Before questioning these strangers I had assumed a certain mutuality. I believed that children of survivors were, in fundamental ways, like me. This belief had contributed to my feeling of an immediate kinship whenever I had met children of survivors in the past. The illusion of similarity extended to their parents as well. I assumed that I recognized their parents because I was familiar with my own. I presumed other children of survivors related to the Holocaust as I did. I learned this was not necessarily so. I was surprised to find that the Holocaust was not a part of the ongoing, conscious life of some children of survivors.

During the interviews I attempted to hide my own feelings for fear of influencing the subject's responses. But I was aware of many instances of tears welling up in my eyes as I heard descriptions of survivor parents and their experiences both during and after the Holocaust. In some cases I recognized family dynamics and individual conflicts as similar to my own. Frequently, a respondent would articulate a theme that I had been aware of subliminally through most of my life but had never clearly enunciated. I learned a great deal about myself through the disclosures of my volunteers.

The agony of our parents did not end with their liberation at the close of World War II. Their legacy of pain and changed personalities dramatically affected a generation that never saw an SS storm trooper. This book is an attempt to clarify the effects of that legacy on their children, actors involuntarily grafted onto this ignominious period of human destruction.

1

The Psychological Profile of Survivors

> He who has been tortured remains tortured. . . . He who has suffered torment can no longer find his place in the world. Faith in humanity—cracked by the first slap across the face, then demolished by torture—can never be recovered.
>
> —Jean Améry

To understand the children of Holocaust survivors, we must first become familiar with their parents' responses to their own experiences. The psychological aftereffects of the survivors' trauma are often mirrored in the attitudes, perceptions, and fears of their offspring. Many children of survivors await a repetition of the persecution their parents experienced. Their homes were shaded by ominous clouds and peopled with ghosts and demons.

Survivors of the Holocaust, particularly Jewish survivors, are often seen as a unitary phenomenon by both mental-health professionals and laypersons. And yet the experiences of individual Jews during World War II varied markedly. Some Jews spent most of the time in hiding, and some eluded capture by posing as Gentiles, with forged papers as proof. Others lived in ghettos and concentration camps for periods of varying duration, while thousands more were exiled and confined in work camps in the Soviet Union. A handful fought in the forests as partisans.

Most survivors (particularly those who lived in eastern Europe) experienced the murder of immediate and extended family members.

Many lost a spouse or children. But some were lucky enough to have retained a mother, a father, sisters, or brothers. Obviously, survivors' personalities during the prewar years were as disparate as those in any large group of people. Significantly, the war and subsequent persecution caught people at different ages and developmental periods.

All these variables shaped not only the survivors' reactions during the Holocaust and their postwar adjustment, but also, by implication, their manner of future parenting. Survivors differed in the degree and kind of emphasis they gave to the Holocaust in their postwar families. Some parents talked of their experiences and impressed on their children the importance of memory. Others avoided mention of the Holocaust years and attempted, as best they could, to obliterate its influence on their later lives. Some survivors turned away from their Jewishness out of fear or anger. For others, their continuing Jewishness became inextricably bound to the horrors witnessed in the past.

In 1964, after years of clinical experience in diagnosing and treating concentration camp survivors, William Niederland, a psychiatrist, published a landmark study proclaiming the existence of a "survivor syndrome." He listed a host of symptoms manifest in individuals who had survived Nazi persecution: chronic anxiety, fear of renewed persecution, depression, recurring nightmares, psychosomatic disorders, anhedonia (an inability to experience pleasure), social withdrawal, fatigue, hypochondria, an inability to concentrate, irritability, a hostile and mistrustful attitude toward the world, a profound alteration of personal identity, and, in many cases, hallucinations and depersonalization (an alteration in the perception of the self so that the feeling of one's own reality is temporarily lost).[1]

Leo Eitinger, a psychiatrist and Holocaust survivor who had extensive clinical contact with many concentration camp survivors in Norway and Israel, observed a similar survivor syndrome:

> The most predominant sequel to the concentration camp activity seems to be the deep changes in personality, a mental disability which affects every side of the personality's psychic life, both the intellectual functions, and especially, emotional life and the life of the will, with the many facets of difficulties in adaptation and the complications which this leads to in the victim's life. Chronic anxiety states, often provoked by nightmares and/or sleeplessness at night, by disturbing thought associations and memories during the day, chronic depressions of a vital type, inability to enjoy anything, to laugh with others, to establish new,

adequate, interpersonal contacts, the inability to work with pleasure, to fill a position—in short, the inability to live in a normal way—are among the most characteristic symptoms of this condition.[2]

Niederland's and Eitinger's reports focused attention on a group of individuals who, in many ways, had been forgotten. Moreover, Niederland and Eitinger asserted that persecution left lasting, perhaps permanent, effects on the survivors. The conclusion of the war, the liberation of camp inmates, and the resettlement of refugees had not meant an end to the effects of the Nazi atrocities. The studies by these two men became the point of departure for most psychiatric pronouncements about survivors.

Subsequent articles by other professionals reported a variety of other symptoms and advanced similar explanatory theories. They stated that the intense depression survivors felt led to complete social withdrawal, seclusion, and profound apathy. Survivors were overwhelmed by indelible and grotesque images of death.[3] They isolated themselves because they believed that no one could understand or appreciate the horrors they had been through. A sense of alienation ensued.

Survivors, these writings asserted, would forever have difficulty establishing any close relationships. They had lost a basic trust in people because of their own persecution and because they witnessed the physical and mental deterioration of their parents. Unconsciously, they maintained a fierce anger because their parents had been unable to protect them from such devastation. Furthermore, it was hypothesized, survivors had difficulty "reinvesting in life" and were deeply ambivalent about founding new families.[4] They would not allow themselves to become emotionally attached because they feared another precipitous separation.

Some studies reported that the emotional responses of survivors had a pervasively shallow quality. "Psychic numbness" or "psychic closing off" were terms used to describe survivors' inaccessibility to feelings. During the Holocaust, while they were experiencing the overwhelming losses and stresses and the resultant intolerable anger or fear, survivors blocked out all capacity for emotion in the interest of continuously adapting to their changing, hostile environment. Although this defense was valuable at the time, its lingering deployment was obviously maladaptive.[5]

Psychosomatic symptoms such as ulcers, hypertension, and premature aging emerged among many survivors who would not allow themselves an emotional catharsis. Some researchers concluded that survivors' massive repression of wartime memories resulted in their generally blunted ability to feel. Contradicting these assessments, other clinicians reported that their survivor patients ruminated excessively about their Holocaust experiences, were preoccupied with mourning, and were generally hyperemotional. Some were subject to fits of violence, as previously suppressed rage, too dangerous to express at the time of persecution, emerged. In psychiatric writings about survivors, contradictory findings abound.

Perennial depression and anger in survivors may have resulted from their failure to engage in "grief work," the necessary mourning of losses. During the war, they had been unable to afford the luxury of that letdown. After the war, they faced the pressures of adapting to a new country, new language, new customs, and new responsibilities. Many desperately wanted simply to get on with life once again, and they believed "others" were not interested in their Holocaust experiences or their traumas. Describing what he referred to as "death immersion," one investigator proposed that many survivors had been so inundated with death that they were unable to mourn their losses fully.[6]

"Survivor guilt" is the name given to a phenomenon frequently reported by social scientists, who have offered various interpretations of its origin and function. Survivors may blame themselves for not going to greater lengths to save others. One researcher wrote: "They have a perpetual need to atone for cowardice or other 'failures.' There is either real personal shame or assumption of collective shame for the failure of Jews to fight the Nazis."[7] Primo Levi, a survivor of Auschwitz, noted: "When all was over, the awareness emerged that we had not done anything or not enough against the system into which we had been absorbed. . . . Consciously or not, he (the survivor) feels accused and judged, compelled to justify and defend himself."[8]

A survivor may be haunted by the thought, "What right did I have to live when better individuals than I died?"[9] Indeed, he may believe, on some level, that his life was made possible by the death of others. "Are you ashamed because you are alive in place of another?" Primo Levi writes. "And in particular, of a man more generous, more sensitive, more useful, wiser, worthier of living than you? . . . It is no more than a supposition, indeed the shadow of a suspicion: that each man is his brother's Cain, that each of us . . . has usurped his neighbor's place and lived in his stead. It is a supposition, but it gnaws at us; it has nestled deeply like a woodworm; although unseen from the outside, it gnaws and rasps."[10]

Survivors may castigate themselves for misconduct they engaged in during the war in order to subsist. Levi stated, "Coming out of the darkness, one suffered because of the reacquired consciousness of having been diminished. Not by our will, cowardice, or fault, yet nevertheless we had lived for months and years at an animal level."[11] This behavior may have reinforced the notion that one was indeed worthless and deserved to die—an apparent internalization of the Nazi image of the Jew.

From a more psychodynamic viewpoint, survivor guilt may reflect the constraints against the expression of rage toward the perpetrators of his misfortune, toward the Nazis and their collaborators, and toward parents who failed to provide protection from those torturous events. Instead of expressing rage outward, however, the survivor turns it upon himself. And, finally, survivor guilt may serve to motivate an individual to bear witness to the Holocaust and continually remember those who were murdered.

For some clinical observers, survivor guilt plays a central role in the development and perpetuation of the ensuing symptoms of social withdrawal, depression, preoccupation with the past, and fear of persecution. Proof is offered in the assertion that after liberation, survivors appeared to be relatively free of symptoms as long as they believed that family members might be alive. Some even experienced a feeling of triumph at having made it through. It was only after deaths had been confirmed that these self-destructive features emerged. Another explanation offered for this symptom-free interval is that survivors were desperately directing their energies and attention to beginning a new life; having children, however, reawakened repressed conflicts, especially those concerning the loss of loved ones, the expression of aggression, autonomy, and control.[12]

When asked, "How did you make it through?" most survivors answer, "Luck." For in addition to acknowledging that many stronger and craftier people did not last, those who did experienced countless close calls, made split-second decisions based on little information, and witnessed the death of others who were less fortunate. The attribution of luck may, however, have subtle implications. If one believes one is alive simply or mostly because of luck, one may live with an uneasiness, a fearfulness. Just as one was given life by chance, something just as capricious may snatch it away.

A legacy of the Holocaust that has recently received some attention involves the often ill-fated marriages survivors entered into after the war. Most of these commitments occurred soon after liberation, perhaps too soon. They seemed to be motivated by a desire to avoid the mourning process and/or to replace lost family members immediately (there was an unusually high birth rate in the displaced-persons camps of Germany that housed refugees). Some of the most precipitous marriages occurred between survivors one or both of whom had lost a spouse or child during the preceding years.

All too often, love was not the driving force behind these unions. An awkward social leveling frequently occurred.[13] Survivors disregarded the usual criteria (educational level, life style, previous socioeconomic status, degree of religious observance, and so on) in choosing a mate. Instead, they chose partners who had endured similar experiences during the Holocaust (for example, being in a concentration camp, a ghetto, a work camp in the Soviet Union, or a partisan group) or who had resided in the same city or neighborhood before the war. They believed that such persons were the only ones who could possibly understand what it had been like during that long nightmare. (Interestingly enough, a sense of being understood by a survivor spouse is not necessarily based on the recounting of one's life during the Holocaust. On the contrary, in many marriages, survivors know relatively few *details* of their spouse's experience.) The partners in such marriages often reinforced feelings of persecution and victimization in each other, and an unusual quality of mutual dependence or protectiveness frequently ensued.

A survivor's memory of a first spouse and perhaps child who were killed often overshadowed the new family indefinitely, producing an even greater awareness of the anomalous or peculiar nature of the new marriage ("If there had been no Holocaust, I never would have married someone like you"). These unions were frequently characterized by a lack of closeness, at best, and a hostile stalemate at worst. Both spouses tended to concentrate their attention on and derive pleasure in life from the children rather than each other.

Marriages of survivors to "nonsurvivors" (those not directly exposed to the horrors of the Holocaust) often met a similar or worse fate. Nonsurvivors frequently expected the symptoms present immediately after liberation (especially those affecting the relationship) to disappear eventually and were disappointed when they lingered. Because survivors tended to believe that anyone who had not undergone the circumstances of the Holocaust could not possibly understand what it was like or what it did to a person, they felt that nonsurvivor partners could never understand them. The upshot was withdrawal and noncommunication.

Many marriages between a survivor and a nonsurvivor, of course, were very satisfying to both partners. Oftentimes, the nonsurvivor was unusually supportive and protective of the spouse, prompting a closeness enhanced by the complementary empathy of the nonsurvivor and the emotional needs of the survivor.

Some reports have suggested that those survivors who waited for a few years before marrying developed more satisfying and pleasurable unions than those who did not. Their choice of a spouse was less desperate and more likely to have been based on positive qualities that could provide the foundation for a happier future. Perhaps these individuals also gave themselves time to mourn before attempting to rebuild a family structure.

In recent years more sophisticated and controlled research has identified various factors affecting postwar survivor adjustment. A person's pre-Holocaust personality and the type of persecution to which she was subjected during the years immediately preceding World War II may affect later psychological problems. People who were children as opposed to late adolescents or adults during the war appear to have more internal obstacles to establishing emotional ties with others. A child's personality was not only less developed in a global sense, lacking in adequate coping mechanisms, but that very basic establishment of trust that must occur in the first few critical years of life was retarded. Such persons may make up the most vulnerable group of survivors, especially as they approach middle age.[14] The younger a child was when persecuted and separated from parents, the higher is his or her risk of later personality decompensation, according to some evidence. Sole surviving members of families seem to have more difficulties than those left with other close relatives. Survivors subjected to sexual assault may experience more extreme psychological disturbance as well.[15] Finally, some reports suggest that female survivors display more disturbing aftereffects of the Holocaust than do their male counterparts.[16]

Differences in survivors' wartime environments and in their specific experiences (witnessing a parent or child killed, for example) may account for differences in later adjustment. Some researchers have attempted (naively, I believe) to quantify the stress in these various conditions and correlate it with the present symptoms of survivors. Any *potential* effects of particular stress on a person, however, will always depend on that person's *perception* of the stress, as well as on his or her coping skills and defense mechanisms. Therefore, it is not surprising that a recent study of a nonclinical sample of survivors indicates that later symptoms are not necessarily related to the particular circumstance in which the individual was victimized.[17]

Three other factors are important in understanding the survivors' postwar reactions. The first is their own perception or interpretation of their ordeal. For example, do they engage in any self blame for their family's plight? Do they feel guilty for having abandoned parents? The second factor is the prolonged period of time they suffered, often with no end in sight, as distinct from other massive trauma victims (for example, Hiroshima survivors). The Holocaust-related persecution of Jews was also unusual in the perpetrators' attempts to subject their victims to continuous humiliation, producing an attitude of unworthiness in some that may have contributed to protracted self-hatred and/or rage.

Communication about Holocaust experiences is more likely to have taken place in families where both parents were survivors than where one of the parents was a nonsurvivor. Also, parents who had an opportunity to strike back actively during the war, as, for example, partisan fighters, are more likely to have related their experiences to their children. This retaliatory posture may have imbued these individuals with a certain sense of pride which subsequently motivated them to relate their past history. Conversely, those who perceived themselves as having breached certain moral imperatives may have been more reluctant to remember or confide previous behavior.

One psychiatrist characterized some survivors as "suspicious of counterfeit nurturance."[18] Having witnessed a morally inverted world where the righteous were destroyed by the power of evil in man, these survivors developed an intense distrust of human beings and human relationships. Only family members, they believe, can be counted on. And even they may falter in their fealty.

After the war, most survivors went to either the United States or Palestine (later, Israel). The very different nature of these havens may have also influenced their future life. According to some reports, twenty or thirty years after the close of World War II, survivors who settled in Israel displayed fewer pathological symptoms than those who emigrated to North America. Perhaps they were able to identify their own rebirth and rehabilitation with the rebirth and growth of the state.[19] Israel also afforded survivors an opportunity to develop positive self-images as pioneers building a homeland and refuge for Jews. The precarious military situation allowed an outlet for personal anger in action supportive of a national cause, with the subsequent victories over the Arabs providing a boost to self-esteem damaged by past feelings of helplessness and loss. The continuing perilous situation in Israel helped survivors focus their attention on an outside group and, therefore, may have prevented their being preoccupied with themselves. Furthermore, Israel has provided opportunities for supportive mourning outlets—special programs and commemorations on Holocaust memorial days, the museums and educational centers at Yad Vashem and Kibbutz Lohamei Hagetaot. The outward expressions of grief and aggression available in Israel may have forestalled the hostility that some survivors directed toward themselves.

Despite the Ashkenazi and Sephardic clashes of culture and physical appearance that European Jews encountered for the first time in Israel, the refugees of the Holocaust were more likely to feel at home in this Middle Eastern country than in America. They were among their own. They could more easily identify with the Jews in Palestine, who also had it tough. Despite its reputation as the "Goldena Medina" (the Country of Gold), America was a gentile and, therefore, potentially hostile land. Jewish refugees could not feel at home with American Jews, who seemed to know so little of what had taken place in Europe and often seemed to care less. American Jews were perceived to have always had it easy, while the Jewish refugees now had to struggle again after all they had endured.

Research design problems have always plagued conclusions concerning Holocaust survivors. Despite the assumed general similarities of trauma—the disruption of family ties and familiar environment, the exposure to a world gone mad, the witnessing of murder and torture, personal debasement, the annihilation of individuality, the continuous terror of standing on the threshold of death—most studies have not differentiated the effects of diverse wartime experiences. Because of the overlap in observed symptoms, some prominent theoreticians aggregate survivors of the Holocaust, Hiroshima, and Vietnam when writing about the aftereffects of those calamities. A few investigators have, mistakenly I believe, narrowly focused on the neurobiological determinants of later abnormal behavior, citing the frequency of nutritional deprivation, head injuries, and chronic infectious diseases suffered by many survivors.[20]

Most studies have also failed to consider the contribution of prewar personality characteristics in individuals' coping mechanisms during the war or in their adaptation after liberation. One often-quoted social scientist in Israel asserted that he found absolutely no evidence of prewar pathology in the families of survivors.[21] This assertion, of course, was based on retrospective reports of survivors, who, we know, often tend to idealize their prewar existence. But why should we not expect to find the same incidence of pathology in these families as we would find in families of the general population at that time?

Perhaps this view was partially motivated by a desire to counterbalance those who have attempted to minimize the heinous behavior of the perpetrators of the Holocaust and, therefore, its potential for psychological trauma. In 1954 the West German government enacted legislation designed to make possible reparations to those who suffered during the Holocaust. In order to qualify for those payments, however, survivors had to undergo extensive medical and psychiatric evaluations, usually by German-born physicians. The burden of proof rested on the survivors, who had to establish a causal connection between their present symptoms and previous persecution at the hands of the Nazis. The West German indemnification office (Entschädigungsämter) often denied applicants' claims because of a neatly imposed self-absolution created by the German medical community: the symptoms of survivors were attributed to their faulty *Anlage* (constitution). These doctors proclaimed that survivors would not have developed problems had it not been for their infantile neuroses, which made them excessively vulnerable to stress. William Niederland objected vehemently:

> The etiology of these conditions has all too frequently been attributed to the "Anlage," the constitution, to other events, indigenous factors . . . to something which went on between the survivors and their parents during their first and second year of life. It seems hard to believe that the four or five years in Auschwitz, with total or almost total family loss, the

complete degradation to the point of dehumanization, the chronic starvation and deprivation of everything human, are considered incidental factors, so to speak, in fully stated medical psychiatric opinions for the courts.[22]

Although psychological difficulties were noted as early as 1947 from interviews conducted on the island of Cyprus with refugees who had been prevented from disembarking in Palestine, most of the initial observations of survivor symptoms occurred in the 1950s and 1960s during examinations designed to assess the merit of reparations requests to the German government. Because German-born physicians usually conducted these examinations, the survivors may have been selective in what they chose to mention. For example, survivors reported fewer psychological and more somatic problems to the German physicians than they did to social scientists in more neutral, scientific interviews. Physical symptoms were more tangible, less easily denied by the enemy. With more neutral questioners, survivors talked significantly more often about feelings of mistrust, hatred, and isolation.

Still, the most widespread distortions in the composite picture of survivors have occurred not because of survivors' perceptions of hostility in examiners but because almost all mental-health professionals conducting their psychotherapy operated from a psychoanalytic viewpoint, notorious for its emphasis on and assumptions of psychopathology. These therapists often generalized falsely about the *group* of survivors from single dramatic case studies or impressions derived from contact with very few patients. Theories about human behavior usually demand generalizations, a selective blindness to individual differences, a leveling to a common denominator, oversimplification. One psychotherapist wrote, "These victims show a submissive, compliant, and always fearful attitude, since they are still afraid of punishment and retaliation from authority figures." While this description may have been valid for a particular patient, it is not true of all or most victims of the Holocaust. A prominent psychiatrist in Los Angeles described the concentration camp inmate's behavior as "sadomasochistic regression." The Jew's masochistic needs, he wrote, *provoked* the sadistic impulse of the SS. A typically neat psychoanalytic pathological complementarity. Another analyst stated:

The acceptance of the slave role may become a permanent characteristic of the survivor, some of whom act as though they have never been liberated. In a few cases, we found a severe inhibition of intellectual function, memory, and interest in anything outside of work and home routines . . . a complete compliance with the picture of the slave laborer permitted to live only if he worked and blindly followed orders, without manifesting any interest or action of his own.[23]

It is my impression that proportionately very few survivors have sought any form of psychotherapy. Those who have, may, therefore, be an unusual sample of the group. Several investigators compared survivors not in psychotherapy with individuals of similar geographical background and age who were not personally exposed to the Holocaust. Their findings indicated that these survivors experienced a poorer sense of well-being, a more pessimistic attitude toward life, and a greater orientation to the past.[24] These symptoms were not as severe, however, as those reportedly seen in clinical samples of survivors. Survivors who coped reasonably well after their traumas would not have come to the attention of those spinning theories about their postwar psychological adjustment.

Unfortunately, subsequent professionals in contact with survivors readily accepted the notions of early observers. These assumptions were repeated as gospel, and later theories were based on previous, shaky theoretical foundations. One of the best illustrations involves Bruno Bettelheim, perhaps the most widely known and most often quoted writer in the field, who was imprisoned in Germany in 1938 and released before the war began. In an almost condescending manner, he described (in contrast to himself) Holocaust survivors collectively as a regressed, submissive group whose captivity resulted in a loss of dignity, humanity, and self-assertion, and whose later life bears the scars of that psychological regression which took place in the concentration camp. The survivors' dependence and regression, which Bettelheim decried, led to a final identification with their Nazi captors, he asserted.[25]

Bettelheim used the dynamic "identification with the aggressor" to explain the cruel behavior of the Kapo (a prisoner in a concentration camp who was granted the privilege of being a guard over other inmates) toward other prisoners. The Kapo, according to Bettelheim, had, in a sense, capitulated. In an environment that supposedly caused an individual to regress to a childlike dependence on his captors, the Kapo now aspired to be like the SS, while, at the same time, accepting and incorporating their notion of him as a contemptible object of derision.[26]

There is, however, a good deal of evidence to the contrary. The most malicious of Kapos appeared to be the "green" tagged prisoners—those incarcerated for having engaged in previous criminal behavior. The "red," or political, Kapos were generally more humane in their treatment of others. The "green" Kapos, therefore, may have simply been exhibiting a cruelty and aggressiveness already present before their incarceration and not one simply engendered by the camp environment.

> Who became a Kapo? It is once again necessary to distinguish. The first to be offered this possibility, that is, those individuals in whom the Lager commander or his delegates (who were often good psychologists) discerned a potential collaborator, were the common criminals, taken from prisons, to whom a career as a torturer offered an excellent alternative to detention. Then came political prisoners broken by five or ten years of sufferings, or in any case morally debilitated. Later on it was Jews who saw in the particle of authority being offered them the only possible escape from the "final solution." But many, as we mentioned, spontaneously aspired to power, sadists, for example, certainly not numerous but very much feared, because for them the position of privilege coincided with the possibility of inflicting suffering and humiliation on those below them.[27]

Contrary to Bettelheim's cynical description, much attestation suggests a great deal of helpfulness between camp inmates. Many survivors of the camps readily admit that without the opportune advice, emotional support, or physical help of their compatriots, they would not be alive today. Many prisoners unquestionably pretended to imitate their masters in order to curry favor, while not necessarily wanting to inflict punishment on others. Finally, to have truly regressed in a camp meant death. Survival required a hyperalertness to changing circumstances, an active manipulation of the environment, the employ of all of one's interpersonal acuity and craftiness.

Most psychiatric professionals interested in the "post-traumatic stress" of the victims of persecution, have assumed that Holocaust survivors require a corrective psychotherapeutic experience. Almost immediately after liberation, most survivors turned their attention to renewing and rebuilding their shattered lives. Therefore, on an emo-

tional level, psychotherapy would afford these individuals an opportunity to engage in the mourning process they had previously
sidestepped, and an arena in which they could safely ventilate their
repressed rage.

Writing about the required cognitive changes during psychotherapy, prominent psychotherapist Yael Danieli stated:

> Cognitive recovery involves the ability to develop a realistic perspective
> of what happened, by whom, to whom, and accepting the reality that it
> happened the way it did. For example, what was and was not under the
> victim's control, what could not be, and why. Accepting the imperson-
> ality of the events also removes the need to attribute personal causality
> and consequently guilt and false responsibility. An educated and con-
> tained image of the events of victimization is potentially freeing from
> constructing one's view of oneself and of humanity solely on the basis of
> those events. For example, having been helpless does not mean that one
> is a helpless person; having witnessed or experienced evil does not
> mean that the world as a whole is evil; having been betrayed does not
> mean that betrayal is an overriding human behavior; having been vic-
> timized does not necessarily mean that one has to live one's life in
> constant readiness for its reenactment; having been treated as dispens-
> able vermin does not mean that one is worthless; and, taking the painful
> risk of bearing witness does not mean that the world will listen, learn,
> change, and become a better place.[28]

And yet, it has been the rare survivor who has sought any psychological assistance. Resistance to treatment emanates from many different quarters. Some survivors may fear the transformation of a self-
image predicated on a feeling of the uniqueness of one who has
survived and conquered death to one who is mentally ill, from one
who is unusually strong to one who is damaged. These individuals
may, at times, extend this feeling from one of uniqueness to one of
superiority in comparing themselves with those who did not suffer the
horrors of the Holocaust, or even with those who suffered, but in
"milder" circumstances.[29]

Because of some survivors' powerful need to forget past humiliations, they react by demonstrating an exaggerated intolerance for
human weakness. Only the weak or debilitated need psychological
help, they believe. They may also unconsciously fear being blamed by
the psychotherapist for particular actions or for their inactions during
the war. Authority figures, even in benign settings, arouse anxiety.

Survivors had to make many agonizing decisions and engage in many activities "because of circumstances" that would create moral dilemmas for them in normal times. Perhaps partly because of this internal conflict and partly because of the disbelief and disinterest they encountered when they tried to recount their stories after the war, most survivors became convinced that no one (including any psychotherapist) who did not live in the midst of the Holocaust could possibly understand the motivation for their situational behavior or the psychological effects of those experiences.

By admitting any continuing serious emotional damage, survivors would have to confront the possibility that the effects of the Holocaust might be transmitted through them to the next generation of their own children born after the war—another victory for the Nazis, and loss for themselves. When a survivor recently spoke before one of my classes, she was asked by a student, "Do you think that your experiences have in *any* way affected your postwar family?" She replied, "Absolutely not. My husband and I have always been very strong people. Or else we could not have survived in the first place. Our children were always happy and healthy. One is a lawyer, the other is a doctor, and they have both done very well."

Finally, some survivors are motivated to continue their suffering as a means of bearing witness, providing a personal monument to the six million who did not survive. Their persistent pain may also demonstrate an allegiance and provide a vehicle for the preservation of ties to their lost family.

For the few survivors who choose psychotherapy, the process may be particularly difficult. Psychotherapy requires a willingness to take risks, be open, and, therefore, allow vulnerability. This "basic trust," so essential to the success of the undertaking has, in many cases, been previously shattered by wartime psychic losses. Survivors may have an exaggerated concern about losing control, about relinquishing defenses they see as critical to their present stability. Distortions of memory are commonplace. Prewar family life tends to be idealized. Some patients demonstrate an inability to remember past events, particularly those associated with feelings of guilt (and subsequent embarrassment) or humiliation.

Potential pitfalls for psychotherapists include an inability to remain objective in the face of their own feelings of rage or despair upon hearing the horrors they had previously believed existed only in fiction. Conversely, they may be unable fully to appreciate or believe the experiences presented to them, and their skepticism will consequently be communicated to the patient. Worst of all, they may attribute the patient's present symptoms to unresolved childhood conflicts and give scant credence to the impact of Holocaust experiences per se.

While the mental-health community, writers, and artists have focused their attention on the pathological inheritance of the Holocaust, they have rarely acknowledged or credited the strengths residing in survivors that have not only enabled them to pick up the shattered pieces of their lives but in many cases have resulted in more than adequate postwar functioning. One reason for this failure to note the positive adjustment of many survivors may be the fear of permitting the denial of the severity of the trauma. After interviewing survivors in America, one typical observer wrote that because the survivor-immigrants were pessimistic, apathetic, excessively anxious, and unable to concentrate, he did not believe they would be able to work effectively. Yet we know that most survivors worked diligently and did well financially, usually rising rather quickly to middle-class respectability.

This adaptation occurred despite disappointment and significant additional stresses after liberation. After the Nazi hegemony ended, many survivors began the search for family members who might have eluded or outlasted their persecutors. In the overwhelming majority of cases, that search became fruitless and depressing. Escaping to the West was for many survivors another frightening, stressful ordeal.

In addition, after liberation, survivors imagined they would be embraced by the world. In fact, many returned to their homes to encounter hostility and confiscation of their property by the local population and, in some areas (for example, Poland), spontaneous pogroms by their anti-Semitic neighbors. Displaced-persons camps in Germany were usually woefully inadequate, their barracks and barbed-wire perimeters reminding many refugees of a concentration camp existence they had assumed was over. Upon immigrating to a new country, with its foreign language and unfamiliar environment, survivors were further brutalized by a world that clearly did not comprehend or care to hear about what had transpired in Europe. Many survivors therefore felt compelled to present a false sense of well-being, thus reinforcing their feelings of alienation from the "normal," nonsurvivor world. By contrast, the ameliorating effects of a supportive environment must not be underestimated. Norwegian survivors, who returned home to a psychologically and materially helpful community, showed fewer traumatic aftereffects than survivors in other countries.[30]

In the United States and elsewhere, survivors raised families, started businesses, went to movies, danced at weddings, and assimilated a new culture. In short, they lived, at least outwardly, much as their neighbors did. A few attempted to derive a higher-order meaning to their survival and were driven by a sense of mission to bear witness or to establish a strong Jewish homeland. Most who felt a debt, however, repaid it with their dedication to carry on and live life as normally as possible for their own sake and the sake of their children.

Indeed, in furthering our understanding of human behavior, we might fruitfully investigate the resilience of survivors instead of simply focusing on their debilitation. Given the horrors and degradation to which they were exposed, how did they go on and function in a *relatively* normal manner? What life-enhancing mechanisms asserted themselves in the face of such physical and psychological devastation? Why didn't most survivors, particularly those exposed to the worst elements of the Holocaust, escape to a psychotic world, one in which they could assert control and deny what they had witnessed and endured? The keys to this mystery might open the door to entirely new realms of human capacities.

Many survivors see themselves as "not normal" and forever scarred by their wartime experiences. They mourn the loss of their former selves and former lives. Survivors in general, however, do not perceive themselves as being stunted or damaged in their ability to function. The degree of psychological problem they manifest, the intensity with which they long for an idealized pre-Holocaust life, and the extent to which they dwell on wartime losses and experiences to explain continuing bouts of despondency are all probably affected by the lives and families they were able to reconstruct. Some have been more fortunate than others in the material wealth they have accumulated, in the *naches* (joy) they have derived from their children, in the work or professional lives they charted for themselves, in the relationships they have established.

We must consider the future of the survivors. As most enter old age, a phase characterized by reintegration, reinterpretation, and reminiscence, trauma that had been successfully buried may come to life.[31] An alarming sense of futility and despair may emerge if they have failed to tell their stories so that the world will not forget. Doubts may sear their consciences as they question whether they have fulfilled their responsibility to those who were murdered. Additional stresses of old age, both psychological and physical, may demand new coping efforts that overtax depleted reserves.[32] Because older people generally tend to become more isolated, we must undertake conscious efforts to ensure that community support is provided to survivors in this potentially difficult time of their lives.

2

Intergenerational Transmission

"I never forget the Holocaust. I'm always shouldering this burden. I don't know why I can never forget about it. I know it's supposed to be healing to forget, but I'm never really able to do that."

"I have a survivor's mentality. I am very resilient. I know I'll come through situations no matter what."

There was significant diversity in survivors' post-Holocaust adjustment. One would expect that children of survivors, individuals one generation removed from the catastrophe, would, therefore, evidence an even wider range of Holocaust-related reactions. Yet, just as generalizations have been offered to describe a "survivor syndrome," so too, many investigators have adopted an assumption of the *inevitability* of transmission of pathology from survivors to their children.[1] It is asserted that because Holocaust experiences negatively affected the survivor's capacity for human relations, he or she has been unable to be an effective parent and that this disability has had damaging psychological ramifications for children raised by these adults. "It is reasonable to assume," two researchers observed, "that the price of survival for these people may have been deep rooted disturbances within the families they formed after liberation."[2] A psychologist noted: "Given children of survivors' unique interaction with their parents' Holocaust

Epigraphs: these and other unattributed statements that appear as chapter epigraphs are the words of respondents in my study.

history, the development of alternative feelings states and an altered view of social life is to be expected. The survivors' Holocaust experiences are evidence of an unprecedented distortion of human social relations. They inevitably incorporated their experiences into their world view, and passed their perspectives to their children."[3] More specifically, it has been suggested that "based on clinical experiences with such patients (children of survivors) our impression is that these individuals present symptomatology and psychiatric features that bear a striking resemblance to the concentration camp survival syndrome described in the international literature."[4]

Indeed, many children of survivors echo problematic themes. They often display an ambivalence when relating to their parents and the shadow of the Holocaust. Depression frequently results from an over-identification with their parents. On the other hand, those who chose to extricate themselves from their Holocaust-filled environment are prone to feel guilty about having done so.[5] Identification with a survivor parent provides the child with a sense of closeness and understanding. Indeed, relinquishing some of the characteristics (for example, depression, anger) displayed by the parent may be perceived by the self as traitorous. At the other extreme, we find children of survivors who feel that their parents are claustrophobically and myopically obsessed by the Holocaust. (One child of survivors mentioned that she purposefully chose to attend an elite WASP college in order to escape her narrowly focused, Jewish survivor world. Another remarked: "I went out of my way not to be like my parents, not to get sucked into those Holocaust-related dynamics. That's how I survived my family.")

Becoming an individual and abandoning the felt obligation to care for survivor parents have been difficult tasks for many children. Parents may have communicated that they could not endure another separation, even the normal developmental disengagement that must occur between parent and adolescent so that the child may develop an identity of his or her own. Disengagement from children may have elicited feelings associated with previous separations and subsequent loss of family members. Survivors may not have had much empathy for their child's struggle because they had no opportunity to learn how to move away naturally, both physically and psychologically, from their own parents and thus did not experience the importance of that process. Finally, in order to justify their existence and alleviate survivor guilt, some survivors may have encouraged dependence in their children.

At one extreme, survivors became totally involved in their child's life and received tremendous vicarious satisfaction as a result. (At the other extreme, survivors were too preoccupied with their own mourning to attend adequately to their child's needs.)[6] They lived the childhood and adolescence they were denied by the Holocaust. One analyst proposed that survivors view their children as their own resurrected siblings, resulting in a further inhibition of the separation-individuation process.[7] (Typically, children of survivors were named after murdered relatives.) A mistrust of outsiders which permeates some survivor homes may also have interfered with the creation of boundaries between parent and child.[8] From many different quarters, a pattern has emerged of problematic psychological and physical separation from survivor parents.

> The struggle of individuation versus entangled family relations was further indicated in varying degrees by current expressions of guilt. The children openly talked about guilt as a pervasive element covering many aspects of their relationships with their parents. Fantasies of separation or real attempts to separate from the family often evoked powerful guilt feelings since the implicit loyalties would be violated. In the words of a 28-year-old subject: "I used to dream about getting away, traveling . . . but how could I abandon my family? It was a real dilemma being on my own as opposed to being a good son."
> . . . setting one's own life as a priority could be seen as a hostile/aggressive move, on an unconscious level. In its extreme form, this could become associated with primitive fears of abandonment and death, given the nature of the losses already experienced by these families. We can better understand why these children allowed over-involved family relations to continue to counterbalance the guilt generated by natural drives for maturity. Our sample reported perceptions that these close ties were mutual need-satisfying "arrangements" both for themselves and for their parents. Furthermore, they claimed that it was their sense of responsibility toward their parents that caused this type of involvement. This correlates with their earlier descriptions of their parents as more needy and vulnerable than were other adults.[9]

For survivors, their children were symbols of rebirth and restoration. These parents may have harbored unconscious magical expectations that their offspring would undo the destruction of the Holocaust and replace lost family members, provide meaning for their empty lives, and vindicate their suffering. Survivors' children may also have provided the justification for their survival, thereby expiating survivor guilt.[10] The direct or indirect communication of these overwhelming expectations created a need in many children of survivors to achieve a great deal in order to compensate for their parents' deprivations.[11] If they perceive they are unsuccessful in their attempts to offset their parents' losses, they may be left with a disturbing sense of failure, even though the task, in reality, is an impossible one.[12] "The need to discover, to re-enact, or to live the parents' past was a major issue in the lives of survivors' children. This need is different from the usual curiosity of children about their parents. These children feel they have a mission to live in the past and to change it so that their parents' humiliations, disgrace, and guilt can be converted into victory over the oppressors and the threat of genocide undone with a restitution of life and worth."[13]

"I've felt I've been in a low-grade depression throughout most of my life," David, a thirty-year-old Orthodox Jew, admitted. "For years I've had headaches which are not organically related. In my teens I was preoccupied with the Holocaust, Nazis, and taking revenge. I would picture myself walking into a bar, spotting a former Nazi, kidnapping him, and torturing him. I had trouble concentrating in school because of my preoccupation with Nazis and revenge."

Guilt is a recurring theme in the literature describing children of survivors.[14] Some offspring identify with their guilt-ridden parents. Others may experience a need to share in the past suffering of their parents and murdered family.[15] One analyst wrote: "Their [children of survivors] concern with the horrible event preceding their own birth is expressed by a tendency to repeat the suffering themselves."[16] Survivors may have further contributed to their child's guilt by directly or indirectly reminding the child of his good fortune compared with the deprivation the parent endured.[17] As a result, one investigator wrote, "gratification of one's own impulses was complicated by guilt and issues of entitlement."[18]

Guilt and anger are the opposite sides of the same coin. Those made to feel guilty invariably grow to resent that onerous burden. Themes of anger and the mishandling of that emotion have been commonly observed among children of survivors. But the reported explanations and assertions in this realm have been far from uniform and at times even contradictory.

Children of survivors have pointed to their parents' emotional un-availability, lack of empathy, overprotectiveness, and guilt-inducing behavior as sources of their frustration and resentment. Anger at the Nazi persecution of their parents and their extended family of whom they were deprived is another consistent motif found in children of survivors.

Many reports have indicated not only the prevalence of anger in children of survivors but difficulties in its appropriate expression as well. Some children of survivors became overly compliant in order to please their parents.[19] Many children of survivors believe they should not further irritate the festering wounds of their parents, who have already suffered so much.[20] Others deny their anger or project it onto the world, thereby reinforcing their fears of renewed persecution. In a study of young children of Holocaust survivors living on a kibbutz in Israel, one investigator wrote that while he found no conspicuous patterns of psychological disturbance in this group, he noticed that "when confronted with open aggression (from children and adults as well) or with danger of war, the children's tendency is to react passively, to escape, to hide, to cry, to stick to the group of children, and not to respond by active aggression."[21]

Contrary to the above description, some investigators observed that teenaged children of survivors were more likely than their peers to engage in aggressive, antisocial behavior. It was asserted that the parents' depleted energy due to the preoccupation with their losses, and the resulting inflexibility of their responses, made it difficult for them to control their children.[22] It has further been proposed that children of survivors are somehow prompted to manifest the anger their parents have found difficult to articulate directly.[23] "The children of concentration camp survivors may become the transferential recipients of parental unconscious and unexpressed rage. The survivors, being terrified of their own aggression and unable to express it, may broadcast explicit or implicit cues for their children to act it out."[24]

Mistrust of others is another difficulty often found in children of survivors. Survivors, angry and suspicious of the non-Jewish world, reinforced these attitudes in their children. (A few offspring reacted to this constricted outlook by embracing Gentiles and nearly avoiding Jews.) This process, along with their status as immigrants, may result in some children of survivors living with a "sense of uncertainty, and separateness."[25]

Survivors' guarded approach to a potentially hostile world has invariably led them to be overly protective of their children. Having stood at the entrance to death, perhaps on many occasions, survivors continue to feel unusually vulnerable. This "death anxiety" is the source of repeated warnings of impending danger.[26] Relatively innocuous, everyday activities may be perceived as lethal hazards. Children of survivors may react to this apprehension by developing excessive, unwarranted fears of their own. The vulnerability felt by the parent infects the child. By contrast, some children of survivors attempt to unburden themselves of their parents' smothering yoke and consequently engage in frequent combat designed to assert their self-confidence.[27]

Survivors' protective and often intrusive style of parenting may not simply be a reflection of their Holocaust experiences and losses. Their relationship to their children may be modeled on family norms they experienced growing up in Europe. These norms emphasized the primacy of the family and inculcated in the child a sense of obligation and deference to parental needs. It is difficult, therefore, to ascertain which, or how much, of these two influences have determined this particular survivor-family dynamic.

Because their grandparents, aunts, uncles, and cousins perished during the war, children of survivors are aware, in a very tangible way, of the odds against the birth of the new family to which they belong. This realization and their parents' frequent pointing to luck as their savior in their close brushes with death may significantly contribute to a feeling in the children of survivors of being special; moreover, the children may assume the identity of survivors as though they themselves had been persecuted by the Nazis.[28] One child of survivors remarked, "I have a sense of being different. It's a miracle that I am here to begin with."

Feelings of marginality have also been observed in children of survivors. One factor contributing to these feelings may be the constant reminders of their families' immigrant status—their parents' difficulty with English, the immigrant friends and relatives with whom their parents almost exclusively socialized, the different norms and expectations present in their homes as compared with those of their American peers. For some children, an overly protective attitude toward their parents may have interfered with the establishment of intimate relationships outside of the home.[29]

Many children of survivors report the intrusion of Holocaust imagery in their everyday life, sometimes triggered by external stimuli, at other times spontaneously springing from the recesses of their psyches. Whatever the source, these images serve as a powerful organizing influence and reminder of one's identity as a child of the Holocaust: "For example, a young woman sees 'the big guy on the subway' who says, 'Hey, don't push me man,' and his image makes her think of Nazis and a common 'strength and cruelty and violence' of which she says, 'they all kind of come together and I have a tremendous fear of all of them, a very vulnerable feeling.' "[30] One female child of survivors wrote of her own demons:

> In school, when I had finished a test before time was up or was daydreaming on my way home, the safe world fell away and I saw things I knew no little girl should see. Blood and shattered glass. Piles of skeletons and blackened barbed wire with bits of flesh stuck to it the way flies stick to walls after they are swatted dead. Hills of suitcases, mountains of children's shoes. Whips, pistols, boots, knives and needles. . . .
>
> Burglars and murderers—the words came in a pair—were always at large, liable to break up a party or disrupt my class in school or even take three thousand people out of Carnegie Hall. They would storm through the doors in their black boots and jackets, shoot their guns or just point them at people, shouting, 'Out! Quickly!' until everyone had filed out and the place was empty.[31]

Survivors, more than their offspring, are prone to unrealistic and excessive reactions to seemingly innocuous stimuli. Authority figures in uniform and dogs are the most common symbols likely to arouse anxiety from a previous time. Items or situations associated with parts of survivors' lives of which they were deprived may evoke sadness. Unfortunately, as children, their offspring did not understand the connections that elicited the outbursts by their parents and often became unduly frightened themselves both by the stimulus and by their parents' fragility. Some may even have felt responsible for a parent's reaction, assuming their behavior had caused it, since no other readily understandable provocation was apparent. Thus they may have come to feel guilty and inhibited about any expression or behavior that might further upset the delicate balance of their parents' adjustment. One child of survivors described the following scene:

> I remember stretching up high to hold my mother's hand as we walked to the school to collect my two older sisters, one of whom was in kindergarten, and the other who was in second grade. As we rounded

the corner, my mother would suddenly grasp my hand almost fre-
netically, and I would sense terror in her. I could not define this at age
three, but I would find out much later what forces were operant. . . . My
mother explained to me that as we walked to the school in Gary, Indi-
ana, she would catch sight of the steel mill's smoke stacks and suddenly
be seized with the fear that those ugly, gray billows of smoke emanated
from crematoria . . . like the ones in which her parents and family were
destroyed.[32]

There are striking parallels in the flawed nature of the approach
to research with survivors and their children. As is the case with
survivors, reports concerning their children have, for the most part,
emerged from psychoanalytic quarters, with, therefore, an implicit
and overdetermined focus on pathology. Analysts have described an
almost all-encompassing plethora of symptoms (depression, guilt,
phobias, delinquency, sexual dysfunction, assertion problems, separation anxiety, anorexia nervosa, psychosomatic problems, gender
identity confusion, conflicts concerning intimacy) that they have observed in their patients. In order to understand symptoms observed in
children of survivors, analysts have drawn intricate hypotheses to
explain the transmission process between parent and child, such as
narcissistic and protective identification, the projection of masochistic
tendencies onto the child who is forced into the role of executioner,
and the reactivation in parents of a negative oedipal complex based
upon their ambivalent relationship with the SS.[33]

By recognizing these methodological difficulties, I do not mean to
imply a mitigation of the lasting impact of the traumas suffered as a direct result of Holocaust experiences. My purpose is to caution against
the unwarranted assumptions and facile generalizations that produce
oversimplifications, a denial of individual differences, and a hyper-
vigilance to similarities in the promotion of "theories" of human dynamics. If there were no "phenomena" to discover and describe, social
scientists would lose their raison d'être. The process may, then, become cyclical as authors attempt to demonstrate the degree to which
their findings are consistent with previous clinical descriptions.

Decrying the unsound methodologies of reported studies and the
concomitant unjustified generalizations that have emerged from them,
one researcher wrote: "It is patently clear that these clinicians assumed, from their psychoanalytic perspective, that psychological
damage *must* have been perpetrated upon the children, and then

proceeded to search for evidence to confirm their impressions. . . .
Are there no Holocaust intact survivor parents who foster and create
warm, loving home environments? If one were to be persuaded by the
symposium participants, one must conclude with the unsupported
and unnecessarily pessimistic response that they do not exist."[34]

One of the most vexing dilemmas we face in attempting to understand survivor adjustment, survivor-child dynamics, and the survivor
child's perceptions of her parents is ascertaining the contributing effects of Holocaust trauma versus the stresses experienced by survivors
in the course of rebuilding their lives after liberation. The people
whom I interviewed frequently questioned whether their parents'
behavior or their own was more likely a result of their status as an
immigrant than because they were a survivor family.

For example, many children of survivors described their feelings of
protectiveness toward their parents. Even as a youngster, they would
be the one to make telephone calls, ask directions, write letters, in essence "front" for the parent. One investigator wrote, "Children of survivors acted as caretakers to their parents."[35] Might not this be the case
in immigrant families of many different ethnic backgrounds? Might,
for example, the child's perception of the survivor as emotionally
unavailable, inflexible, and controlling reflect an eastern European
parent's familial expectations? Raising these questions, of course, does
not imply a denial of the problematic symptoms or themes that charac-
terize survivors or their children, but we must question our assumptions of etiology.

Reports by clinicians on the psychological problems transmitted by
survivors to their children seem to be rife with methodological problems and incongruent data. One observer noted the presence of more
anxiety in children who had one survivor and one nonsurvivor parent
than in those from two-survivor families.[36] Another wrote that the
length and severity of the survivors' Holocaust trauma may have
directly influenced the transmission of pathology to their offspring.[37]
Another researcher found that the potential for problems in the child
depended upon the degree of trauma experienced by the survivor, so
that, for example, if both parents were in a concentration camp (the
most stressful condition, he assumed), the child was likely to be less
educated, have greater impulse-control problems, experience more
interpersonal difficulties, manifest more depression and anxiety, and
seek psychotherapy more than his counterparts who grew up in a

home in which the survivor parent spent the war in hiding or partisan activity or other less traumatic situation.[38]

Another report indicated that the number of surviving members of the parents' families, the proximity of those family members, the degree of trauma experienced by the parents during the Holocaust, and the extent of family discussion were all inversely correlated with evidence of psychological problems in children of survivors.[39] Contrary to these observations, one social scientist, Zoli Zlotogorski, found no support for a "child of survivors syndrome" and no relationship between the level of ego functioning of children of survivors in his sample and the duration of parental interment, the number of extended family members who survived, or the amount or type of communication about the Holocaust within survivor families.[40]

Perhaps it is unrealistic to expect a clear understanding of the transmission process that occurred in survivor families. There are simply too many factors to consider. Many of the variables that may have affected the parent-child relationship have already been elucidated. Others quickly come to mind. How many years after liberation or after immigration was the child born? Had the survivor already had time to acclimate to a foreign environment? Was the child the firstborn? If so, did he absorb the brunt of the parents' excessive expectations, "European mentality," and vestiges of Holocaust-related fears, thus making it easier for subsequent siblings?

Almost all studies of the transmission process rely on the child's *perception* of her parents' behavior and attitudes. Researchers seldom have the opportunity to see these families in action; and when we do, it is at a moment of crisis and at a particular point in the unfolding life of both parent and child. Yet we know that children frequently learned little (or at least do not remember much) of their parents' Holocaust years, particularly the more gruesome, horrific, and embarrassing details. We know, too, the potential for distortion in the recollection of parents' stories, which almost surely inspired anger, guilt, or awe in the hearers. And we must assume that the child's genetic temperament and her world outside of the home significantly influenced who she is today. We note the different quality of relationship with parent, the different attitudes toward the Holocaust and Judaism, the different values and life styles adopted by siblings brought up in the same survivor household.

Most studies of children of survivors, particularly those published in the 1960s, 1970s, and early 1980s, have described adolescents and young adults. For example, one clinician reported that his children-of-survivor patients expressed feelings of alienation and isolation and exhibited a weak sense of identity.[41] Would these features be true of many teenagers who are going through the exceedingly difficult transition phase between childhood and adulthood, particularly those teenagers we see in psychotherapy?

And then we come to those studies that purport to find no striking psychological differences between children of survivors and their respective peers in either the United States or Israel.[42] Many of these investigations attempted to control for such crucial variables as European background and degree of religiosity. The greater number of reports from Israel than the United States that indicate no unique difficulties in the adjustment of children or survivors perhaps reflects the easier adaptation of survivors who emigrated to Israel. Perhaps, too, like their parents, children of survivors were less likely to feel "different" while immersed in a Jewish state with its particular emphasis on heroism and its outlets for aggression.

In the 1960s, several clinicians noted that children of survivors composed a disproportionate percentage of adolescents treated in psychiatric settings.[43] In a study of seventy-one children of survivors ranging in age from seventeen to twenty-nine, one investigator reported that approximately 18 percent of his subjects had been in some form of psychotherapy.[44] In fact we do not know what proportion of the tens of thousands of children of survivors has sought psychological assistance. No one has questioned a random sample of hundreds or thousands who comprise this group. In addition, of course, many individuals, no matter the background, who experience emotional difficulties do not avail themselves of treatment. Nevertheless, a majority of those who participated in my study—and whom I believe are a fairly representative cross section of children of survivors—had at one time been in psychotherapy. This high figure was undoubtedly influenced by the educational level of this group. Research in the general population consistently confirms that higher-educated individuals are the most likely to have been in psychotherapy, not necessarily because they exhibit more psychological problems but because they tend to be more introspective than their counterparts who have had less schooling.

Children of survivors are extremely diverse in their personality profiles, their levels of achievement, and their life styles. Previous generalizations about this group have often been founded on a blatant disregard for the rules of scientific inquiry. The number and complexity of seemingly relevant factors may render impossible clear and concise explanation. Two investigators summarized the pitfalls:

> It is precisely the nature of second generation survivor status, including the fact that the parents' actual experiences and transmission of these experiences encompassed a wide range, that results in diversity as a major outcome. Further, the mechanism of second generation effects is seen as an extremely complex one in which the cumulative trauma of parental communication, the aspects of the parent-child relationship determined by the Holocaust context, and the historical imagery provided by the parent and by other cultural processes are mediated by interaction with normative developmental conflicts, family dynamics independent of the Holocaust, variables of social class, culture, Jewish heritage, and immigrant status.[45]

> Attempts to make causal connections in terms of the outcome in the offspring of the effects of parental traumatizations is problematic because of the complexity and large number of interacting individual variables that are involved. These variables relate to the pre-trauma personality of the survivor parent and the nature of the Holocaust traumatization, the age of the survivor to the trauma, when losses of family members occurred, loss of previous spouse and children, whether both parents are survivors or only one, the personality of the nonsurvivor parent, the degree of survivor syndrome pathology in the parent, additional trauma acting directly on the child in his or her early years . . . the psychosocial conditions in which the child grew up, the extent of formative influences outside the home, parents' communications with the child about their Holocaust experiences with regard to content and style, and so on.[46]

Notwithstanding the multitude of potentially relevant factors impinging upon the development of children of survivors, certain themes seem to be apparent in many of these individuals despite their diversity in personality and adjustment. And while we may not precisely understand the transmission process from one generation to the next, we do find common motifs, sensitivities, and conflicts in this population. There is obviously a matrix, an atmosphere that has permeated the development of children of survivors. And while this atmosphere may have affected different children in different ways, I am convinced after reviewing all the exchanges in my interviews that its influence was inescapable.

The experience of being a child of a survivor is reflected by three words uttered by almost every such person with whom I came into contact: fear, mistrust, cynicism. While a few described their mistrust or "paranoia" as "low level," most saw these three elements as having produced significant difficulties and colored their outlook on life. The world, for these children of survivors, is clearly a hostile protagonist.

Some survivors directly and repeatedly impart to willing listeners their firsthand observations of man's savagery. Human nature is malevolent, and this malevolence is especially directed toward Jews. The world of the survivor's past as well as the one he presently inhabits is a dangerous one. Many children of survivors learned this lesson well. Ironically, as we shall see in a subsequent chapter, some of the distrust that their children experience results from survivors' emotional unavailability and their lack of empathy with their offspring. Furthermore, a few of the children of survivors I interviewed believed the source of their cynicism to be attempts on the part of their parents to hide their present feelings and Holocaust history.

Sitting with me at her dining-room table late in the evening, Sheilah, a thirty-eight-year-old mother of two, offered her view of the world.

> I learned the world is a scary place. It's best to live in a world that is very small and like you, not to trust anyone who isn't Jewish. I'm a very fearful person. I don't believe it when someone says that everything will be okay, that I'm safe. I was in Acre [Israel] once with several girlfriends. There were many Arabs around, and suddenly I was seized with an irrational fear that I would be raped by them. My girlfriends tried to tell me everything would be okay, but I wouldn't believe them. It wasn't true that I would be safe.
>
> I also tend to be a very pessimistic person. I won't drive to an unfamiliar place because if I am lost and I ask for directions, I assume the directions will be wrong, sometimes even that the person has intentionally given me wrong directions. The world just can't be trusted. I consider myself a nervous person and I think it's directly related to the Holocaust.

Beverly, a thirty-year-old elementary school teacher, spoke of what she learned from her mother and father.

> Knowing the gruesome details of their experiences must contribute a little pessimism to my nature, a more cynical outlook on life and what my fellow man is capable of than people with more normal family histories would have. They (my parents) taught me not to trust people.

Emphasize the dress, the appearance, the external. The way you are is not necessarily okay, so present a false picture of what people want to see.

I carry a deep sadness in my life. The Holocaust has increased my awareness regarding the dark side in us—because we are mostly machine and animal. There are very few human beings. My mother would say, "There are a lot of Hitlers out there so you've got to be tough."

It is mind boggling, terrifying to realize the destructive nature of man. Some perpetrators of the Holocaust did not set out to murder and destroy. Some murdered unquestionably. The former perpetrators also came to be murderers without remorse. That it can and did happen leaves disturbing implications on my outlook on life. I cannot be so trusting or idealistic. . . .

For the most part, I have come to realize that you cannot depend on other people. Only a few people will really come through for you when push comes to shove, so you must always look to protect and succor yourself. . . . Life can be a hostile environment, so if you can maintain a confident inner self, you'll be in better shape. I think I am like my father in this way.

"I have a strange mix of cynicism and optimism," remarked Ruben, a thirty-six-year-old physician. "The extreme horrors and cruelty of the Holocaust color my view of the political and bureaucratic world. I view all statements and promises by all authority figures with suspicion. On the other hand, my parents' examples of surviving and reestablishing lives after unimaginable terror and destruction serves as an inspiration."

Mathew, a thirty-year-old painting contractor, noted that his mistrust resulted from what his parents did *not* communicate. "I realize that my long time inability to trust others or express myself in a meaningful way is directly linked to the confusion I had due to the experiences I had growing up in a family where so little attention was paid to the realities of what my mother experienced during the war."

Herb, a thirty-eight-year-old radiologist, spoke of the source of his qualms.

The Holocaust has scared me, wounded me, at best. I'm a fearful person. My mother, because of her overprotectiveness, instituted a sense of mistrust, that the world is a dangerous place. She always reminded us to be on the alert to real or imagined dangers—making sure no one was following you, making sure you look around when you come home at night. There were constant reminders to check the doors and windows to see if they were locked. Even today when my brother or I leave to travel anywhere, especially if it is by airplane, there is an attempt to dissuade us from going and instead stay close to home.

"I'd consider myself a hard-core realist," Fran, a professor of business administration, wrote. "There is an ugliness to life that I understand at some level, even though I was raised in a middle-class home. I paint no rosy pictures of people and the world. At times I've been more cynical and have made attempts to overcome that. I think the Holocaust has also contributed to a low-level sense of paranoia."

Paul, a forty-one-year-old attorney, described a pessimism prevalent among children of survivors.

> I'm politically cynical. I feel the people in power are abusers of power. I don't expect kindness and am generally pessimistic in my worldview. . . . When I have resentments, they generally occur because I'm afraid of being taken advantage of. I feel the universe is indifferent. I have a real self-centered view of the world. I need to get what I can for myself because I fear that it can be taken away at any time. I don't think that we can do very much to save the world and all we can do is make ourselves and our loved ones happy. Happiness I don't really believe is possible. We can only do the best we can for a little while and then we die and that's it.

The imagery invoked by Benjamin, a thirty-six-year-old physician, was, perhaps, the most dramatic I had heard: "My parents avoided Judaism. They were frightened. On the one hand they tried to assimilate and I have tried to assimilate. My ex-wife and present wife are not Jewish. I have continued my parents' need to assimilate. Yet they also had a need to hold onto their ethnic Judaism. Keep your Judaism but don't let others know. Cut off your foreskin but keep your penis in your pants."

Children of survivors voiced a wariness of their fellow man and a bleak view of human nature, which resulted in their guardedness with others, a reluctance to be honest about their thoughts and feelings, and an expectation of being taken advantage of, both psychologically and physically. Some participants spoke of a more generalized apprehensiveness as well.

> "As a child, I was a very fearful kid. I always worried something bad would happen. I've had to fight to overcome this during my

life. . . . My relationship to others is less naive because you know what other people are capable of. We learned you have to choose friends carefully, that you can't trust people. When I was a child I wasn't an open person. I always had this lesson drummed in that you can't trust people, only your close family. . . . I've always had a need for security—both physical security (having locks and alarms on the doors) and financial security. My dad always said, 'Get educated because that can never be taken away from you.'"

"I have a fear of authority. Policemen make me particularly nervous—but really anyone who represents authority or has my life in their hands. I live with a sense of doom, that something bad is going to happen. I don't trust anyone who isn't Jewish. I see the world as black or white. There are good people and bad people. I think this is partly due to the dichotomy of Jew and evil Nazi. . . . When I watch a movie and there is a moment of danger when the outcome is uncertain, I just can't take it. I'll literally walk out of a room."

"I get anxious easily. As you can see, I'm a stutterer. My mother is a very anxious person. I'm a fearful person. I have intense highs and lows. I overreact to bad and good things. I'm frightened that tomorrow's not going to work—in my marriage, my career. I think that's directly related to the Holocaust. Victims wondered, 'What's going to happen tomorrow?' Goyim don't live like that. They don't worry about tomorrow all the time. That's part of my attraction to them."

Since most survivors speak of luck when explaining their good fortune at having outlived the Nazi menace, it was not surprising to find that their children viewed life as precarious, unreliable:

"I believe that *anything* can happen and that *everything* does happen. In other words, the human being has the ability and willingness to destroy others totally."

"I am very appreciative for the life I have. I know how fortunate I am. I also try to remember to live for each day. Also, what we have we can lose very rapidly."

"Basically I'm a sad person. There has been lots of depression in my life to which I think the Holocaust has contributed a lot. So much of my life had undercurrents of terror. It's like being an abused child without the abuse—that awful things were about to happen. What's going to happen tomorrow? Things are going too well. Something bad has got to happen next. I have a gallows humor which reflects this as well."

"My Holocaust background has made me look at life as a hard, constant struggle, an ordeal. There are always obstacles to overcome."

Several children of survivors described a continuing undercurrent of apprehension. They have adopted the role of victim with its attendant perception of persecution. Michael, a thirty-two-year-old accountant, illustrated this theme:

I think that I bought into the image of being easily victimized. This has undoubtedly affected my self-confidence. A victim's mentality sometimes causes me to quit before I've started. I'm not going to get what I want anyway. Bad things happened to my family, so why shouldn't they happen to me? I would attribute this to my mother saying, "If there wasn't a Hitler, we would have x." So I identify with her losses. I have a sense that I will always lose and I continually have to fight that even though I try not to let it get the better of me.

In the course of our conversation, another child of survivors remarked, "I live with a certain insecurity. I think I'm afraid of being found out on different levels."

As noted earlier, guilt and depression are common motifs manifested in the offspring of survivors. Guilt for not being good enough. Guilt for growing up in easier circumstances. Guilt for feeling anger toward one's parents. Guilt for inflicting further pain on a survivor. Parents themselves have induced some of this guilt with such remarks as, "How could you do this to me after all I have suffered?" In other instances, children have assumed the characteristics of their parents.

Mark, a thirty-four-year-old jeweler, spoke of the pressures he experienced:

I have a tremendous need to succeed. I feel like I always have to prove myself. My parents had to *kvell* (shake with pride). They were always speaking of other children of survivors and compared them with me.

I have a fear of abandonment, of rejection. I remember as a kid feeling as though I had to be a good boy. I was always very compliant because if I weren't people would be angry with me and then they wouldn't want to have anything to do with me. I always put other people's needs, especially my parents' needs, first. I just couldn't do *anything* that might hurt them.

I had known Harry, a businessman of thirty-five, since childhood, although our relationship had never been a close one. I did not know about his mother's history nor his reactions to it.

My mother is very critical and judgmental. My parents always had a black/white, right/wrong view of the world. No gray areas. I think it's a result of their Holocaust experience. When the ghetto was liquidated, my mother and her baby were taken with her mother-in-law to a concentration camp. When they were lined up for death or life her mother-in-law said, "Give me the baby. You'll have more babies." So she gave her baby up. My mother is racked with guilt about having given up her daughter. I found out that my mother has taken the birth date of her daughter as her own. Because she was so self-critical, she was always very hard on others. I became very hard on myself as a result. I have a lot of guilt, starting with bringing home a bad grade from school when I was in the second grade.

Steve, an actor, spoke of his darker side, which he attributed to his Holocaust background.

I am a pretty depressive guy with wide mood swings. When things are going well for me, I am tremendously guilty. Psychologically I think I have a built-in will to fail. There's a lot of self-loathing in me that is similar to my mother's self-hatred for having survived. I am expected to do well. I have the potential to do well, and at the same time I do not deserve to do well.

I always felt responsible for my parents' unhappiness, so when I am with a lover, I am overly threatened when they are unhappy. I feel that somehow I'm the cause of it. This makes me secretive and unwilling to communicate my feelings, particularly when there is danger of upsetting my loved one or causing a scene. When there are problems I hide them because I'm too guilty over the pain my revelations would cause my mate. I think this is because of my Holocaust background. I was always reluctant to "rock the boat" and upset my parents because the degree of their discomfiture was more than I could handle. With my lovers I have projected that their response would be the same, so consequently I avoid any controversies. . . .

I was the center of my mother's world and I always think first about myself, or think the world thinks of me first. This manifests itself in extreme shyness and awkwardness around people. I always assume that they notice everything I do, and that they are always judging me. It's as if people have nothing better to do at parties or the workplace than to notice and be affected by my presence—usually in some negative way. I take everything personally. If I don't get a job it's because I'm no good. I am just super self-critical.

While fear and mistrust were the most common difficulties described by children of survivors, distancing oneself from one's parents and establishing a separate identity were also frequently mentioned as problems. The basis of this predicament was usually the survivor parent's overprotectiveness or intrusiveness in his child's life. (I also found in several mother-daughter dyads a desire on the part of the survivor to live vicariously the adolescence that had been denied to her.) The exaggerated sense of responsibility for the emotional care and sustenance of their parents often felt by children of survivors further inhibits the individuation process. A few respondents pointedly referred to the isolating effects of their parents' defensive shield.

"I've had trouble setting boundaries in my life. If someone needs something from me, I must give it to them. My parents tried to live through me and my sister. There was an invasiveness in terms of my privacy. We were their reason for living, so Hitler would not win out. So we have *their* purpose in the world. It was communicated to me that I couldn't trust my own judgment and instincts and had to check everything out with them first. Yet, contradicting this was their telling me I could do anything I wanted. It's just that they didn't want to separate from me. Sometimes I felt like I was my parents' parents."

"They [my parents] lived vicariously because their teen years were taken away from them. They were learning and experiencing as we were learning and experiencing. They didn't understand a lot of what we, American teenagers, went through. They were strict European parents. . . . I always felt that I didn't have the same adolescence as my friends. When I went to a friend's house, we went into her room and closed the door. When we were at my house, we wound up sitting in the living room with my mother. I think it's because she didn't have a chance to have an adolescence, so she enjoyed hers through me. She also didn't understand that I would have a need for privacy."

"I have always felt a tremendous responsibility to make my parents happy, since they went through such a horrible experience. It has been difficult for me to separate from my family. I've always maintained somewhat of a physical and emotional proximity. I have always tried to please my parents and acted as a caretaker, protector to them."

"My parents' overprotectiveness caused me to be isolated as a child. I wasn't allowed to do what the other kids my age were doing. And when I was given permission, there were usually conditions and restrictions. Even today, when I go out to dinner with my parents, I have to call them as soon as I get home or they start to get nervous. You know the Jewish telegram joke, 'Start worrying. Details to follow.' That's my mother."

In addition to exploring their problematic areas, I asked the people I interviewed if they would at least partially attribute any of their psychological *strengths* to their Holocaust background. Because of their orientation to pathology, previous investigators have, for the most part, failed to present a more balanced picture of children of survivors, although a few social scientists have pointed to their high achievement levels.[47] In a study comparing children of survivors with first-generation American Jewish adults with no Holocaust background, one investigator found that, as a group, the children of survivors in his sample were significantly more likely to have a career in the professions than were the children from the nonsurvivor population.[48] Of course, a high level of accomplishment does not preclude the presence of psychological difficulties, although pronounced impairment would likely be a hindrance to its achievement.

Other investigators concluded that their subjects were well adapted in general despite their feeling a need to compensate for their parents' losses.[49] Felt excessively, such a need, if frustrated, can produce anxiety. However, compensatory desires may also provide the impetus for growth and fulfillment. It is the intensity of the drive as well as the individual's reaction to its blockage that determines the effect on personal adjustment.

The consideration for the children of survivors, therefore, is whether their Holocaust background will debilitate and constrain them or will be transformed into positive intrapersonal qualities and interpersonal concerns. The answer to this dilemma, both in previous investigations and my own, is equivocal. We have seen some of the Holocaust's detrimental effects on children of survivors. Now let us turn to the more affirmative aftermath.

One attribute of children of survivors I encountered frequently was a compassion expressed on a personal, familial, social, and political level:

> "If I hear about oppression in other countries I feel like it is my responsibility to do something because others stood by while Jews suffered."

> "I think the Holocaust has made me more tolerant. I have a special feeling toward minorities. I am very socially conscious, always concerned for the underdog."

> "The Holocaust has made me not believe in the tyranny of the majority. A whole society went nuts, Germany. So when I'm confronted by a mass opinion differing from mine, I tend to call that to mind to strengthen my resolve."

> "Had I not had such a direct link to the Holocaust, I am not sure I would be so involved in seeking answers to questions I have about evil, about inhumanity. I have become more involved in trying to understand issues dealing with morality and immorality, ethics, justice. I believe we must be aware of the capacity we have as human beings to inflict pain on other human beings. Had the Holocaust not been of such close proximity, would I care at all about injustice in the world? Would I be concerned with the dark side?"

For a minority (ten) of my participants, concern for the oppressed and disadvantaged was circumscribed, limited to the Jewish community. For some, their antipathy was a counterbalance for perceived past indifference to the persecution of the Jews: "Where were *they* during the Holocaust." At times they assumed this indifference would apply in the future, as well: "No one is going to care about Jews. We've got to take care of ourselves." Most of those children of survivors who comprised this group defined the pain and loss of the Holocaust as a very central component of their identity. They also, in many instances, perceived their life to have been very adversely affected by their Holocaust background. Four participants in my study expressed another mitigating factor that inhibited their empathy for other oppressed groups. The essence of their statement was, "The Holocaust numbs me somewhat to other tragedies." Or more forcibly, "There has never been *anything* comparable to the Holocaust." Their intense anger produced a limited point of view.

Resilience was the most common psychological strength described by children of survivors. They had successfully transformed their inherited status as victim to one of survivor, and they took pride in their resourcefulness and tenacity. A close identification with these qualities in a parent was clearly in evidence. Emily, a teacher in a Jewish day school, exuded these characteristics. "I'm great in a crunch. You need me in an emergency, I'm there. My mother [a survivor] is incredibly strong and quick to take charge. I'm the same way." Other children of survivors voiced similar self-perceptions.

> "The Holocaust gives me the strength to try harder, to do well—to honor people in my family whom I never knew but, I know, would have loved me a lot."

> "My Holocaust background helps me to fight and do well because of what happened to them, for their memory. To prove that we are good. Wanting to make my mother happy, knowing what she went through. Knowing that my mother got through it and is a great person—funny, charming—gives me strength. I want to keep her going by my continuing fight. As afraid as I am, I'm not afraid. The worst has already happened."

> "I have a survivor's mentality. I'll come through situations no matter what. In my work I have to be tough. I am very resilient. I think I inherited a feeling of being a survivor from my parents. I am proud that they managed to live through it, and I'm doubly proud of all the times they used their intelligence or their spirit to save themselves from what looked like certain death. Many times in my life, I've come through a tough situation thinking, 'I'm a survivor.' I've also had experiences when a last-minute brainstorm saved the day in some way, and I've thought the same thing then. I know that I can rise to the occasion when it's necessary and get through when things look bleak. There have been so many times that it's happened that I know it's not just coincidence, but rather a strength that I have. I've thought fast and gotten myself out of many scraps. I've also been in several tough or impossible situations with other people, when things looked bad and everyone was ready to give up; somehow, though I'm not a natural leader, I surfaced in those groups and came up with the energy, the plan, the stuff it took to get us through or save the day. I always think afterward, 'Dad would be proud.' "

> "My father tried to instill in us a sense of fearlessness. If you can survive the Nazis, there is nothing to be afraid of. I feel that I can

overcome great odds. Even when things look real bad, I believe
things will get better, even though there may be no rational basis
to it. I think about what my father went through and he came out
real well."

While compassion for the less fortunate and resilience in the face of
adversity were the most common positive characteristics mentioned
by children of survivors, many also described their heightened appreciation for life and their commitment to live as fully as possible. Susan,
a successful painter, was emphatic: "I don't take my life for granted. I
really want to do something, accomplish something. I feel like my life
was a gift so I don't waste it."
Other children of survivors were equally insistent.

"My mother's first husband was murdered by the Nazis, so if not
for the Holocaust I would not be—my mother and father would
have never married. So, in a funny way, I have a sense of responsibility because of the Holocaust—to do well, revitalize the Jewish
people. I can't take my life for granted, it must have purpose."

"The Holocaust has taught me that we will all die sooner or later
and that I want to live each day as fully and as honestly as
possible. So it has turned me into an activist. I do not live a
complacent life. I do not think I am any better or worse than the
next person, but I am willing to take risks, be vocal about issues of
importance to myself and defend the disadvantaged. I feel lucky
that I got the opportunity to live, since my mother could have been
killed in the camps. And so I try to live life to the best of my
ability."

Survivors may have induced guilt with memories of their Holocaust
experiences or used these recollections to control their children—"I
never had that when I was growing up," or "You should realize how
fortunate you are." At times, survivors belittled the concerns of their
children: "That's nothing to get upset about. You don't know what *real*
problems are." Nevertheless, perspective *can* provide an effective tool
in preventing an excessive reaction which would paralyze an individual. Several participants positively noted their use of comparison to
summon their psychological and physical reserves. "If I have a problem in life," said one, "I think about my parents' Holocaust experi-

ences. That helps put my problems in what I consider a better perspective—they simply don't seem as awful."

As is the case in most homes, children of survivors acquired both detrimental and life-enhancing qualities from their parents. While many survivors were overly protective, attempting to bind their family together in order to reduce their anxiety, their children grew up with an enhanced sense of closeness to their immediate and extended relatives. Similarly, while many children of survivors were burdened with the task of compensating for losses endured during the Holocaust, they also grew up with an appreciation of the importance of familial continuity. A few children of survivors may feel weak in comparing themselves to their heroic parents, but most have adopted the survivor's resilient characteristics.

Although most of the respondents in my survey cited the Holocaust as the primary influence in their life, diversity abounds in the degree to which children of survivors believe their Holocaust background has determined their personality and choices. But how are we to understand those who deny any personal impact of their family's Holocaust history? Are we simply to take at face value the disavowal I heard from a few children of survivors: "But the Holocaust happened to my parents. I don't understand when you say you want to know how it has affected me." How are we to evaluate the description offered by another investigator of his interviews with several children of survivors? "Individuals often contradicted themselves, for example, simultaneously denying any effects of the Holocaust on their relationship to their parents while affirming a perception that their parents had been permanently and massively affected."[50]

Some children of survivors fled their Holocaust environments, which they described variously as "smothering," "paranoid," "controlling," "guilt-ridden," and "xenophobic." Others embraced the Holocaust as a badge of honor. Their status as "survivors" (albeit one generation removed) made them feel special. Apparently, still others, however, were determined to reject any notion of exceptional status with all the perceived suffocating obligations which that position implied.

Denial is a defense mechanism commonly used to repress feelings of powerlessness and the fear that ensues. Fear, as we have seen, is perhaps the most prevalent problem in children of survivors. One clinician described a group session which included such an individual:

His parents had just barely escaped the concentration camps in time. They were never incarcerated, but he knew in detail of their near capture, and grew up in a neighborhood close to several survivor families. He is a physician, age twenty-eight, and is seen as a tough and unfeeling person, both from his wife, his own report, and the perception of others. He began the interview with the stern statement: "I don't have any feelings about their experiences because I didn't have them. My parents' experiences haven't affected me at all!" As the session progressed, this man became progressively overbearing, verbally disagreeing with others, and criticizing particularly one participant, a twenty-year-old woman whose both parents were survivors. Suddenly he burst into tears and admitted that he remembered this particular person, and how she and her family continually frightened him as a child. He stated that, "They looked like walking corpses with their stark eyes and bones coming through their skin." He saw this girl as also "very pale, extremely skinny and frightening." He continued to describe other families of concentration camp survivors who always intensely frightened him, as *his* parents "could have been caught" and he "could have" looked like the children of survivors whose visions continuously threatened him. . . . It seems likely that as a boy, his pity for these people turned into hate and rage, because he could not successfully deny his fear that it *could* have happened to him. In fact, he reports being preoccupied with these feelings, and during early adolescence attached himself to an elderly Jewish scholar, and began an intensive study of Jewish law and history. According to him, "I read everything where a Jew could get power." . . . According to his statement, he had never before this interview realized fully or ever expressed his childhood fears, and had no previous insight into the important connection between the impact of the Holocaust and the course of his life.[51]

Many children of survivors feel hurt by the Holocaust's lasting effects. They are angry because their parents were emotionally unavailable, or unempathic, or overbearing. Yet, they believe they must repress these feelings because the survivor has already suffered enough. A blow from the child, the repository of so many compensatory hopes and dreams, would be too devastating. Denying the effects of the Holocaust on their development may allow these children to exculpate their parents of any child-rearing deficiencies.

I also have evidence that suggests it may take some time for certain children to arrive at a willingness to examine the effects of their Holocaust background. It may take years of separation from parents before their anger diminishes sufficiently to allow a curiosity and desire for self-discovery to assert itself. A thirty-five-year-old physician, who welcomed my interview as an opportunity "to learn about myself and all this stuff," noted: "I have avoided survivors and their children all my adult life. I didn't want to be part of that community anymore. I didn't want to dwell on this stuff. I thought there was absolutely nothing positive about it." Now, however, he was capable of more dispassionately opening those closed doors he had needed to keep so tightly shut.

3

"For this I survived the camps?"

> "I've never been able to tell my parents about any of my problems. I'm afraid of causing them any more pain. They have no idea who I really am."

> "I am thirty-five years old and I still live three blocks from my parents' home. I tried to move to New York for a year, but the guilt and anxiety were unbearable."

"For this I survived the Nazis? For this I survived the camps?" This was my parents' frequent anguished refrain—if I talked back to them or if I came home later than I said I would without telephoning to report my delay. "For this I went through hell?"—if I went to a peace demonstration and, through no fault of my own, was clubbed by a policeman.

It was as if they had injected guilt directly into my heart. It paralyzed me. How could I answer them back? How could I be certain of the validity of my actions or feelings?

I, my needs, seemed to slip away in the face of their horrible past. Given my understanding of what they had experienced, how could I cause them more grief? How could I electrically prod an already exposed, frayed nerve? How dare I risk the final straw which might precipitate the ultimate psychological breakdown? Their reservoir of pain was already straining the limits of the fragile structure enclosing it. My parents, I believed, were always on the edge. To this day, I find myself reluctant to ask my mother (my father died in 1974) for details of her Holocaust experiences. I much prefer talking with her friends or my more distant relatives, not only about their experiences, but hers as well. I feel too uneasy provoking even a flicker of pain.

At times, I wanted to scream, "You survived because *you wanted to live.*" But this struck me as unkind. It would imbue their survival with selfishness, thus dismissing the nobility of their ordeal. It might puncture their flimsy layer of self-respect. Perhaps they needed to cast their survival in a more meaningful light.

Both my parents would deny any desire to make me feel inordinately guilty. They would recoil from the idea that they made it more difficult for me to express feelings and needs. And they would be deeply remorseful if they understood that I lived in fear of their disintegration and the subsequent ruin of my world. I was not responsible for their past horrors. But I did have the power to agitate, shake, perhaps loosen the floodgate.

I was afraid of my helplessness in the face of my father's explosive anger and my mother's outpouring of sadness. My father had spent much of the war fighting with the partisans in Poland's countryside, exacting his revenge. During that time, he had been task oriented— raining down as much punishment and destruction as possible upon Nazis and local, anti-Semitic Poles. There was no room for tears. I remember his attempts to still my crying when I was a boy. "Fa vus vinst du?" (Why are you crying?) His implication was that I was wasting my time and energy. I only saw him cry late in his life as he emotionally collapsed under the weight of a lifetime of failed business ventures and an unsatisfying, heartbreaking marriage.

My mother's tears, on the other hand, were always easily triggered. Protecting herself with forged documents indicating she was a non-Jewish Pole, she was obsessed during the years of Nazi occupation with being caught, of being found out. She lived in total fear, yet her circumstances necessitated a cool, calm exterior and the presence of mind required to make quick decisions and carry them out. In America, with her life no longer in jeopardy, she could and did drop her armor.

As far as I could see, my friends' homes did not manifest the same tension omnipresent in mine. Our apartment seemed more vulnerable to life's capriciousness. The fact that I seemed to be the only one without grandparents enhanced the difference between my family and others I knew. And, of course, the absence of grandparents meant that another anchor, source of comfort, and evidence of a secure continuity of life was missing.

Acts of rebellion were not a part of my childhood or adolescence. Perhaps this absence can be attributed to my temperament. Under the circumstances, however, I believe it was also a result of a perception of my parents' frailty. My fear of my father also probably buttressed my repression of anger. We spent little time together, he and I. At the end of a twelve-hour day of selling pots, pans, mixers, and cutlery, he would come home, eat dinner, watch television for an hour, and retire to his bedroom. During my formative years he was often peddling his wares for days or weeks at a stretch in distant, rural parts of the country.

I remember him watching Nazi war movies, rubbing his feet together excitedly, his face twitching, and muttering in Yiddish under his breath, "Those sons of bitches." He had a powerful physique in contrast to my skinny, unmuscular body, which added to my fear of his anger, an anger which would erupt if I displeased him. The most frequent explosions occurred because I would not finish what was on my plate at mealtime. A chase ensued, with him yelling and threatening, and me locking myself in the bathroom in order to escape his wrath. He pounded on the door, and I waited for it to fall. If it caved in I knew he would hit me. I could hear my mother pulling him away and telling him to stop.

I mostly sensed my parents' pain and vulnerability. After having learned more details about what actually happened to Jews in Europe, it has been even more difficult to act contrarily, to criticize, to say no. I consciously attempt to augment my empathy. I conjure up the general and the particular details my parents related to me.

Imagine a parent being killed by Nazis.

Imagine parents, brothers, sisters, grandparents, killed by Nazis.

Imagine living for years with the constant threat of death.

Imagine standing at an apartment window in Warsaw, hearing your Polish landlord, who, for the moment, accepts your deceit as a Catholic, upon viewing a Jew beaten and arrested in the street, saying, "I wish they would kill them all."

Imagine going back to your home after liberation and frantically inquiring about relatives and friends. Imagine being told that they were killed, after you had lived for years with hope, irrational as it may have been, for their survival. Imagine feeling compelled to ask for details of their journey to death. "But are you sure?"

Now, imagine that all this happened between my twenty-first and twenty-fifth year.

My parents, particularly my mother, longed for the pre-Holocaust past of simplicity, happiness, close family ties, financial security, skiing, ice skating, sleigh riding in the winter, summer vacations at Krinitsa, an uncle's lap which had to be visited for a few moments every Friday afternoon on the way home from school before shabbos. Life was good to them in Lublin. "For this I survived the Holocaust?" probably echoed their own present unhappiness more than it did their displeasure at my behavior. The mere contrast of pre- and postwar life continued its devastation long after 1945.

And yet I am always confronted with the fact that if there had been no Holocaust, I would never have been born. My mother and father would be married to other individuals. Do the circumstances of my birth imbue me with a particular responsibility? Am I to extract meaning from it? Am I part of the implication of their survival? Is it now incumbent upon me to rebuild two lost families, or perhaps even to deny the obliteration of an entire Jewish people?

Survivors evidence a wide range of involvement in their children's lives. On the one extreme is exaggerated attachment, excessive hovering, and vicarious participation in their offspring's developmental milestones and crises. On the other hand, some survivors are emotionally unavailable to their children, preoccupied with their continuous mourning process, coping with what they perceive to be seriously depleted physical and psychological reserves.

Perhaps the most frequent observation in the psychiatric literature has been the overprotectiveness that characterizes many survivor-child relationships. (Only two studies, both of college-age children of survivors, have not found any unusual attempts to inhibit the autonomy or separation of children of survivors by their parents.)[1] Indeed, when I asked participants in my study, "How do you believe your parents' experiences during the Holocaust affected the way they raised you as a child?" by far the most common and spontaneous response concerned this trait. It was also the most often mentioned difference between the upbringing they experienced and that of their Jewish friends from nonsurvivor households.

Having suffered so many earlier losses and experienced such a dangerous, life-threatening environment, survivors often had inordinate fear that harm would come to their children.[2] Survivors also

implicitly and explicitly affirmed their belief that the world is a malevolent one, that survival, therefore, was provisional. Some survivors
waited apprehensively for the inevitable series of personal tragedies to
extend itself. Their children grew up amid a pervasive scent of vulnerability.

Children of survivors were reminders of loss and symbols of compensation. Named after murdered relatives, they suggested the ever-
present potential for harm as well as the precariousness of those who
escaped the jaws of death and promised to fill the void left by others.
Survivors wanted to guarantee the safety of these vulnerable vessels.
Their need to control their child and his environment might also have
reflected other undercurrents. Feeling guilty for not having done more
to save parents, siblings, or friends, the survivor may have taken a
more active stance in order to undo that failure and diminish past
feelings of impotence. In addition, those who were passive during the
Holocaust perished. Passivity and death, therefore, were inextricably
intertwined. "If I can only keep my child out of harm's way . . ." And,
perhaps, on a more unconscious level: "My parents were unable to
protect me. I must be sure to safeguard my children."

Obviously, one need not be a Holocaust survivor to adopt an over-
protective stance toward one's children. Many parents behave that
way, but in this case the *source* of the attitude is crucial. The child's
perception of the connection between his parents' child-rearing style
and their Holocaust background is central to understanding the second generation.

Joseph and I spoke on the telephone four times before he finally
decided to participate in the study. He would repeatedly ask what the
interview entailed and what areas would be covered and, at the end of
our conversation, would offer to think about it and get back to me.
Eight years earlier, he had been interviewed by a journalist who was
writing an article about the second generation for a newspaper in New
York and had found it a painful experience without any perceptible re-
deeming value. He did not know if he wanted to put himself through
that again. He finally offered to forgo lunch so that we could meet at
his office.

> My mother raised me and my brother in a very protective manner, to the
> point that it was harmful. They did it because they had lost every
> relative. It was their way of guaranteeing that they wouldn't lose their

children. We never had babysitters—never once. My parents never
went out without us.

My brother and I were dissuaded from any team sports which might
lead to injury. When I would ask why I couldn't do most things the
answer was usually, "Because it's too dangerous." I remember being
perplexed about why I couldn't join the Boy Scouts or Cub Scouts. They
weren't seen as Jewish activities. . . . When I was nineteen or twenty I
used to go camping a lot with friends. I had to call home every night. If I
didn't call my mother, she would work herself up into a hysterical state
and she would imagine the worst scenario.

Now a pediatrician of forty, Joseph said, "I came away from this a
very fearful person, a withdrawn child. There were so many things I
wanted to do which were off limits."

My interview with Deborah revealed the potential of parental fear to
resurface in painful experiences for the next generation. Deborah was
thirty-one and had recently remarried. Her first attempt at marriage,
when she was twenty, had failed. She acknowledged that her poor
choice of partner at an earlier age may have been influenced by her
desire to remove herself from her parents' home.

We were overly protected. My mother would say, "Because we've lost so
much, you are so valuable to me." My parents were totally nonreligious,
but, when I was seven, they decided it was time for me to go to Hebrew
School. But there was an intense discussion about whether or not to
raise their children as Jews. They didn't want us to be vulnerable,
visible. They didn't want us to go through what they did.

They always needed to know where I was, when I'd be home, who I
was with, and so on. I had to do a lot of calling while I was growing up.
Even when I was in college and would go back to visit them on vacation,
if I was at a friend's and it was 10:30 P.M., the phone would ring, and we
would all know it was my mother! They also did not encourage sports or
outside activities. They were afraid I would get hurt. There was always
this "fear" which pervaded a lot of activity. If I drove with a half tank of
gas they would be afraid I'd run out and get stuck on the road. Exploring
the environment or the outside world was discouraged.

In so many instances while I was growing up, I saw them being more
worried, more prohibiting, more careful than nonsurvivor parents.
They wanted to protect me from any harm, any danger, any bad influences. As a result, I was not allowed to do things at times that other kids
were doing them, or to go places. They didn't allow me to take new
steps or do things independently until everyone else had been doing the
same thing for a long time—for example, wearing a bra, wearing

makeup and high heels, dating, going out at night with girlfriends, going away to camp, living away during college. They were always a bit more cautious, a little more scared to let go.

My parents held on tighter than other kids' parents. They had to know where I was *all* the time. I remember going to Jewish camp and I had to call as soon as I arrived. I thought to myself, "The other kids don't have to call, why do I?"

They always seemed to fear something else going wrong in their lives. They were also very giving. They will spend any amount of money for us but none on themselves, as if they are not worth it.

I was overprotected and spoiled with love. They tried to remove any chance of suffering. Compared to Jewish nonsurvivor parents, my parents were *always* home for us. They devoted their lives to us—far too much. They still do, and we don't even live in the same city.

They—my parents—held on very tight. To this day they have a difficult time separating. My parents are still terrified of losing my sister and me.

Steve had what looked like a two-day growth of beard when we met. He was, at forty-one, a tall, thin struggling actor and director. I knew he was talented. I had, by chance, seen a play he had starred in at a small local theater.

They were overly protective. Every injury or illness was a cause of major panic and turmoil in the house. They were fearful of most experiences on the outside and were very reluctant to give us permission to do things like play sports or go swimming. I remember once going on a camping trip with four or five other children of survivors. We set up a tent in the woods near a stream and stayed there for a weekend. Only years later did I find out that our parents had gone to the same piece of woods and stayed there hidden over the weekend.

We were smothered with love. "Kim shoen, ess eppes! (Come right away, eat something!)" We were continually fed, burped, stroked, tweaked, and fondled until we were well into our thirties.

Marty was the father of a nine-year-old son and four-year-old daughter. We met one evening in his home. Judaica books and art objects were evident throughout the living room and dining room.

My father does not believe we should "advertise" ourselves. This means he believes we should not make waves in society. For example, he gets very upset when I take part in a public demonstration.

My father was very cautious about allowing us to take chances like other young adults—such as learning to drive at sixteen or staying out late with friends. He believed that we should be good children, get a college education, and become professional people. He does not trust the motives of others, especially non-Jews.

Fear dominated many survivor homes. Fear for the children's welfare. Fear of being victimized. Fear.

Leo, a bespectacled thirty-three-year-old writer for television, spoke with me in his apartment in the hills overlooking Los Angeles. A word processor sat on a desk in the corner of his living room. Dialogue and directions were visible on its screen. We were twice interrupted by phone calls from an agent, which Leo answered apologetically.

> My father's decisions to purchase luxury items and plan vacations were limited even though we could afford it. He believes that one should always plan for the future because a disaster, an illness, a problem, might occur at any time.
>
> My mother raised us to be self-sufficient, prepared, and success-oriented because she was afraid if we weren't self-sufficient, we wouldn't be able to take care of ourselves in case something like the Holocaust happened again. We had to do well to protect ourselves, more than to make ourselves happy.

Marlene, a thirty-five-year-old slightly overweight artist, sat curled on her living-room couch throughout our meeting. Marlene had never been married, and her last serious relationship was with a gentile man with whom she lived for several years. That relationship had caused an ongoing acrimonious debate with her parents.

> My parents always warned us against trusting anyone outside the family—even good friends. We were always cautioned to be careful, not to take risks, to adhere to the rules. Do it the way everyone else did. My parents find it hard to express affection and warmth. There was great emphasis on being safe, finding safe careers, life styles, and friends.
>
> I learned the world is a scary place. It's best to live in a world that is very small and like you. My father is not comfortable being in the spotlight, being visible. He always makes his donations anonymously. I grew up hearing what a hero my mother was, but she was too frightened of the world to go in and speak to the principal of my school.
>
> My mother would not allow her children to put bumper stickers on their cars so no one would know our political beliefs. She would buy only American cars so she would "fit in" better.

Marsha, a thirty-five-year-old pediatrician, was the mother of two boys. She had never spoken about being a child of survivors to anyone before our interview.

> As a child I thought my parents were always angry, yelling at each other. They spoke Yiddish, and I never learned the language because I didn't want to understand. They overreacted to everything. For example, if someone stole a five-cent candy from their store, they became totally paranoid and hysterical. Everything was life and death. They were always waiting for the worst to happen again. I had no way of understanding that when bad things happened to me, I shouldn't take it personally. If someone was late for an appointment, it didn't occur to me that he could have had a flat tire or some other good reason. I always felt, "Why is this happening to me?"—just like my parents did.

Survivors' depleted psychological resources sometimes hindered their attempts to protect their children from imagined dangers and may have resulted in a certain inflexibility in their methods of control.[3] While many survivors were warm and affectionate with their family members, some survivors seem to have discarded the currency of feelings forever. *Do. Keep busy. It's not good to think too much.* Again, it is virtually impossible to assess whether this inflexibility and emotional unavailability had its basis in a pre-Holocaust personality or was a result of wartime experiences.

Perhaps because of depleted resources, survivors frequently resorted to references to the Holocaust and the deprivations they endured as a means of inducing feelings of guilt and influencing their children.[4] "How could you do this to me after all I went through?" survivors frequently implored their children. And as Robert Krell, a psychiatrist and Holocaust survivor, has noted, "Few survivor parents can control their statements comparing the plenty of 'now' and the scarcity of 'then.'"[5] The degree of guilt-inducing communications may be related to the extent of the personal trauma and family losses experienced by the parents, particularly the mother.[6]

"I always thought as a child that my mother never spoiled me," Celia, an elementary school teacher, remarked.

> My mother is a good, pleasant person. But she had such a hard life that she didn't have much to give someone else. My mother never sang lullabies to me as my friends' parents did to them. My father always had health problems because of the camps. As a child, *everything* was con-

nected to the fact that they were Holocaust survivors. "You have to remember that we don't have the strength," or "We don't have the patience because we are Holocaust survivors." I wasn't angry about it. It was simply a fact of life for me. When I told my father, "I'm going to have a child," his immediate reaction was, "That's our response to the Germans. We're going to have another Jew!" They always made us feel extremely sensitive to their stresses.

At thirty-six, Rochelle, a psychotherapist, had finally accepted her parents' limitations, although past frustrations poured out during our interview.

Jewish suffering as a "genre" was held up to me as an implicit diminution of my own personal pain. In other words, the equation was, How can you complain in the face of so much "real" suffering? The result was a home in which the child's psyche was overlooked or belittled; and it created an environment in which I was unwilling to articulate my subjective pain about certain episodes in life.

Their experience invalidated anything I was upset about. Whatever I was feeling didn't count, because if I had pain, they didn't want to hurt. So to shut off their pain, they would tell me it didn't really hurt or I was being silly.

They could not whatsoever relate to the problems of an American adolescent—boyfriends, dating—because theirs was spent in camps. For example, if I was upset about a boy, my mother would berate me for having such insignificant problems. After all, I had food, clothing, a home, and parents. My parents never discuss feelings. They can't cope with their kids being anything less than extremely happy and successful.

Doreen, a court reporter, spoke with regret about being deprived of parental understanding.

My mother is very closed. It is impossible to know what she is feeling. Ever since I was a child I remember you could only have physical pain, no mental pain. You could be physically sick, but you couldn't be emotionally upset. I could never tell her that I've been in psychotherapy.

My mother always said, "You can't sit still. Otherwise your mind will think too much. Women need to cook, clean, bake, sew, and keep busy." My mother is not a warm or affectionate person. There was a coldness in how I was raised. I wanted a mom like other kids had—laughing, full of life. She is very rigid. Things are black and white. I don't think my mother knows how to be sympathetic. I always heard, "I didn't do that or have that when I was a child, so why should you!" or, "You don't know how good you have it. I didn't have those things."

Many survivors displayed an acute lack of empathy for their children's problems and emotional needs, particularly as they compared them with their own. Some survivors focused their attention almost exclusively on external accoutrements and the attainment of financial security in an attempt to quell their anxiety. A few survivors, while being emotionally unresponsive to their children, nevertheless attended excessively to any material or physical needs they felt they might have.[7] They bought their children things. They urged their children to eat.

Marsha, the pediatrician and mother, reacted to her own mother's constricted focus. She was almost anorexic during her teenage years. "My mother's experience with deprivation has made her obsessed with food. I remember having eggs rammed down my throat and vomiting them up, and then having more shoved down again. My mother is always thinking about, talking about, cooking, freezing, or packaging food. As a result, I was the closest thing to anorexic as a child without being one. I didn't really start eating until I went away to college."

Embrace of the work ethic, the quest for material acquisition and financial advancement, the protectiveness of one's children in a new environment often perceived as a hostile one, the desire to control one's children and prevent their separation from family and historical roots have all been fairly typical characteristics of survivors. Still, these attributes also describe many other immigrants. Several of the participants in my study spontaneously offered that they were unable to distinguish the immigrant from the survivor factor while enumerating these features.

As mentioned earlier, a perceived lack of empathy and inflexibility of survivors by their children may also have reflected their new status in a foreign country, their inability to recognize or adapt to American mores. Survivors continued to refer to the standards of the Old World, one which they, furthermore, tended to idealize and simplify, particularly as it concerned familial ties. ("I wouldn't think of saying that [or doing that] to my parent!")

Several investigators have observed that many children of survivors acted as caretakers to their parents.[8] In one study comparing children of survivors with their Jewish peers raised by American parents, the authors noted: "In the course of our study, we were impressed by how frequently 'American' subjects, when asked, 'Have you ever found yourself acting like a parent to your parents?' would say, 'Can you explain what you mean by that?' This never happened with a Holocaust subject; they knew immediately what we meant."[9]

To some extent this role reversal reflected a pattern which we would again expect to find in any immigrant household, regardless of the ethnic grouping. Children "front" for the parents, since they often learn the new language and customs more rapidly. They are called upon to write a letter, answer the telephone, speak with the stranger who rings the doorbell. If a parent has had frightening experiences with authority figures in the old country, this role reversal may also be readily adopted when interaction is necessary with any official representative of a government agency.

The protectiveness described by many of the participants in my study (and reported elsewhere as well), however, included dimensions specifically related to the Holocaust. Many children of survivors were primarily aware of sheltering their fragile parents from emotional distress. They felt a greater responsibility, in particular, to shield their mothers from harm than did their Jewish peers from American families.[10] They were more likely than their American contemporaries to inhibit their desires as they calculated the effect their behavior might have on their parents. Perhaps they had heard, "You will finish the job the Nazis started!" when their activities precipitated parental anxiety.

Perceiving their parents to be overly taxed and permanently traumatized by their losses during the Holocaust, children of survivors often refrained from relating their emotional difficulties, including the usual, normal developmental trials which occurred in their lives. Survivor parents contributed to this conspiracy of silence. Some were preoccupied with their own mourning and failed to hear or see the telltale signs of disquiet. And most survivors had an exaggerated need to perceive their children as happy and problem-free so that they could serve as the requisite compensatory symbol for all that was lost. Their children knew this and played along—though not without resentment.

> "My parents didn't have much education because of the war breaking out. Because my mother was a child (twelve) when the war started, she didn't have a chance to learn things. I taught her

how to dress nicely, set a nice table. She learned those things from me as I grew up and learned them."

"Because my mother endured what she did, I have always felt protective of her. We were always careful not to let her know if anything bad happened to us. My mother was like the youngest child in the family. We felt we had to make her happy in order to make up for all her losses. She lived so vicariously through us. Everything we were living, we also lived for her. It was a shared life. I don't know that she raised us with that intent, but I think that was the result. . . . My mother was always prone to overreact to a particular stress or loss, and I know it wasn't just that event but also because of her past. That's why we won't tell her anything bad. I've known that I can't have a realistic relationship with her. Bad news had to be diluted enough before we would tell her about it."

"As a child I had no needs—other than my parents' approval of me. I tried in every way to please them and protect them. . . . The pictures of me as a child are very serious. I remember clearly my inner heavy feelings as a child. I was afraid of birds. I thought they would drop bombs on me. My close friend was a doll I took very good care of. Emotionally she was alive to me. I gave her my feelings which I could not express or acknowledge in myself. My needs were secondary. First came the happiness and well-being of my parents, especially my mother."

"I've had difficulty with trust, loneliness, and high expectations of what relationships bring. And with anger. I believe that much of this is related to the fact that my mother did not have a traditional adolescence. She was thrown into a completely different existence as a teen-ager, and, therefore, much of what I experienced as a teen-ager was not understandable to her. I, in turn, had to put myself in hiding, as she had during the war."

Perceiving their parents' vulnerability and saddened by their losses, children of survivors justified both their parents' emotional unavailability and the denial of expression of their own needs. This rationalization process, however, had unfortunate consequences. Many children of survivors experienced intense anger because of the impairment of parental functioning and guilt-inducing attempts to control them. At the same time, several investigators have observed that children of survivors had unusual difficulty expressing that anger toward their parents as they tried to avoid inflicting additional suffer-

ing.[11] As a result, the normal guilt experienced by children in response
to their angry impulses was intensified.[12]

Anger presented problems for survivors as well. Because of the
persecution they experienced and the concomitant feelings of powerlessness when they were unable to protect themselves or their loved
ones, male survivors evidenced an even greater rage than their female
counterparts. Yet, after liberation there was no outlet for their fury.
Sometimes, the survivor displaced the anger onto his children as the
frustration generated by the child's behavior triggered the wrath directed toward his persecutors. Unfortunately, the triggering mechanism for this anger was overly sensitive, as the survivor's ability to
cope with additional emotional frustration was already impaired.

Clara, a high school teacher, was familiar with this pattern. "Although my father, overall, raised me well to be a moral and hardwork-
ing individual, I think he lacked some important parenting skills because he didn't have the role models. He is a particularly impatient
person, and this caused me much distress when he attempted in my
early life to help with school work. He was openly and harshly critical
and gave little praise to his children. He had a quick temper and was
perhaps too . . . quick to administer physical punishment—the belt—
when it wasn't warranted."

Emotional explosions and irrational reactions were common in
many survivor homes. Steve became increasingly agitated as he recounted what he had witnessed.

> Hysteria, rage, and anger filled my parents and it all spilled over onto
> us. We were beaten quite frequently; most often when we did some-
> thing that they thought was dangerous or harmful to ourselves. It was
> very common to fall down, hurt your leg and get beaten for it. I don't
> think that would have happened if they hadn't been survivors. If we got
> sick my mother would start crying because we hadn't worn a sweater,
> and my father would beat us.
>
> My father was a stubborn, angry, violent, uncompromising man. To
> this day he doesn't realize there was anything abnormal in his behavior.
> It was always because he had been provoked. By that, I mean it had
> always seemed to him to be an appropriate response to the inappropri-
> ate behavior of his children. He would regret the harm he did but never
> really the actions that caused the harm and sometimes it really did
> border on craziness. A couple of examples. We lived on a chicken farm.
> My brother once dropped a basket of eggs, and my father started chas-
> ing him with an ax. As my brother ran, my father got more and more

angry—now it wasn't because of the broken eggs, it was because my brother was running away from his father. Finally, Dad threw the ax at my brother and hit him with the blunt end between his shoulder blades, knocking my brother down and in the process falling himself and breaking one of his fingers. I remember he got up, marched to my brother and slapped him across the face. He turned to the rest of us and said, "You see what S. did to his father." To this day, he refers to it as the time S. made him break his finger.

I ran away from home once when I was ten years old and Dad chased me down in his car and tried to run me down on the road about a half mile from the house. I jumped into a ditch to get out of the way and he careened over the top of me, crashing into the field. That is referred to as the day I wrecked his car.

Of course, children cannot redeem lives lost during the Holocaust. Still, previous investigators have noted that survivors overvalued their children, perceiving them to represent murdered relatives, if not European Jewry as a whole.[13] Named after a member of one's family whose life was abruptly ended, the child sometimes became the embodiment of that particular individual as well.

> A complex of emotions accompanied the birth of children to survivors. These children were bound to be special. A child was tangible evidence of one's survival and therefore incredibly precious. To some parents the child was the representative or reincarnation of those who were lost; to some the child represented the ultimate defeat of Nazism—a life created against insurmountable odds. And to some, a birth was a profoundly ambivalent religious event, a precious gift from God to parents who frequently no longer believed in God.[14]

To some survivors, children provided an antidote to their feelings of guilt for having survived. Seeking justification for being the one allowed to live, he or she could point to the child and believe, "This is why I survived." At the same time, however, the survivor communicated that the child must vindicate them. Hence, some children of survivors expressed the need to accomplish something out of the ordinary as compensation.[15]

All children are special to their parents. They evoke fantasies and arouse dreams to be fulfilled. However, as survivors searched for meaning, both for their survival and their present life, they often relied too heavily on the gratification they hoped to receive from their progeny. The involvement of some survivors in emotionally unsatisfying marriages made the position of their children more untenable. When a survivor told his child, "You are all that matters to me," he or she may have been telling the truth.

The burden, therefore, on children of survivors could be an unwieldy one. And, because survivors often idealized their prewar life and relatives who were killed, the compensatory hopes became even more difficult to fulfill. The almost inevitable failure of the child to meet these parental needs provoked further depression in the survivor as Hitler's persecution continued and could not be outweighed in the present or the future.

Research concerning sibling position has traditionally noted the greater expectations parents have of their firstborn. Firstborns, therefore, usually have a higher need for achievement as well as greater difficulty separating from their parents. The psychologist Yael Danieli has noted the greater demands for symbiotic devotion and parental fulfillment impressed upon the first child born into a survivor family.[16] This child arrived when the survivor was more depleted and experiencing the stress of a new beginning. Later children grew up with parents who had had more time to adapt to their unfamiliar environment and who were at a greater distance, both physically and psychologically, from the Holocaust. Many children in my survey were acutely aware of the role they played in their parents' life.

> "My parents are more involved in our lives than nonsurvivor Jewish parents. It's more than just a hovering. We've had to make up for all their lost family."

> "We were supposed to be all the people who died. . . . 'We had you for this?' "

> "We were my parents' reason for living. So Hitler would not win out. So we have *their* purpose in the world."

The past suffering and losses of survivors and their continuing sense of vulnerability in a potentially hostile world colored their interactions with their children. They clung to an already decimated family. In Art Spiegelman's book *Maus*, the survivor, cynically and rhetorically, asks his child, "What is friends?" The answer which many children of survivors heard was, "Friends are nothing. Family is everything."

"There was an expressed duty to the brothers and sisters who did not survive. Somehow we had to do better—both in accomplishment and morally—in order to make up for the dead ones. . . . Intermarriage was the major issue. . . . My mother didn't necessarily love my father but she was with him in order to replace the ones who died. She bore the obligation to procreate and replace the six million. My mother let us know that we were always *rebuilding*. There was always that word."

"For my parents, their children's success, especially their son's, is of paramount importance. My best friend is a dentist and his survivor parents are disappointed. It simply wasn't enough."

"My parents' children represented the product of their love, and also the lost lives of their relatives. My and my brother's lives were filled with increased expectations. We were to live our life and another dead cousin's or nephew's or niece's."

Although the interview excerpts here seem to imply a necessarily bleak picture of survivor households, many survivor homes were not oppressively fearful or constraining. These remarks were quoted because they reflected the participants' beliefs of the effects of the Holocaust on their parents. Naturally, therefore, they also mirror the continuing painful repercussions of those events. (No subjects believed that the Holocaust had no effect on how they were raised by their parents.) Another side must be presented as well, however, one which many participants in this survey volunteered.

"Love was a major factor in our upbringing and I believe this was due to the fact that they had lost so many loved ones. There was always a great feeling of giving. Their home was always open to strangers, friends, and family, even when my parents didn't know how their rent would be paid the following month."

"There is a bond that families with survivors have that I believe nonsurvivors don't have. The closeness and love that were given was of a different, more passionate quality."

Recounting the Stories

"When I was taking gross anatomy, I told my father that I just couldn't do it. My father told me a story for the first time. He had lain for thirty-six hours under a pile of corpses in order to hide from the Germans."

"I feel like I'm going to have to ask them about the Holocaust before they die. I've been reluctant to ask because of a sense of guilt. It's too threatening. It causes me anxiety, although I'm not sure why."

The ritual began when I was eight or nine years old and lasted for about ten years. It took place on the night of Yom Kippur. In observance of Jewish legal restrictions, our apartment in Brooklyn was dark except for a shaft of light coming from under the closed door of the bathroom. This streak would be our lantern in the blackness. One was not permitted to switch on electricity for twenty-four hours during this holy period.

The story was brief, always the same. The somber environment and the mystical day on which it was told lent an eeriness to the account. We lay on my parents' bed, my father lying on his left side, I on my right side facing him. I could barely make out the outlines of his face. My father spoke in Yiddish. "We [the partisans] found out that a German officer would be at the farmhouse of a Pole who had betrayed Jews to him. The German was probably delivering the two bottles of Vodka as payment for the two Jews the Pole had handed over. We came in and they were drinking together. We tied them up and cut a small hole in each one's arm. For hours we put salt in the open wound. Then we shot both of them."

My father's voice reflected an increasing bitterness as the story progressed. I absorbed my father's determination as he spoke, and I felt my anger swell. I was fascinated. I was also frightened. I did not ask any questions afterward, and my father did not want to speak anymore. That was what he wanted to tell me. That was what he wanted me to remember.

When I asked children of survivors what they knew of their parents' Holocaust experiences, I again found great diversity in their responses. In part, this reflected the tendency of some survivors to speak openly and frequently about their past while others avoided the subject almost completely. Approximately one-third of the participants in my survey reported that they had heard very little of their parents' history. Another third believed they knew a great deal. Yet, not one person I interviewed could relate a full chronology of their parents' war years. And, after probing somewhat, it became apparent that even those who believed they were quite knowledgeable had failed to learn significant details—such as the name of the concentration camp in which their parent was incarcerated—other than those recounted in the repeated "stories" of the survivor.

Despite the fact that most children of survivors were not well acquainted with their parents' lives during the Holocaust, *all* had a sense of being aware, from a very early age, that they were, indeed, children of survivors.

> "I knew my parents were Holocaust survivors since the day I remember myself."
>
> "I was first aware my father was a survivor when I was in elementary school. I asked him about his KL tattoo."
>
> "The story 'seeped' into my consciousness in an accidental manner since the age of six."

Although a few survivors chose to speak about their Holocaust experiences in public forums—before organizations or educational groups, for example—survivors' revelations to their children were usually fragmentary and occurred over many years. Rarely did a survivor sit a child down and impart a complete account of what had happened to him and his family. Rather, the same events, impressions, or encounters were related repeatedly, so that, in fact very little of that period of the parent's life was truly told. The child's difficulty in remembering his parents' accounts is partly a result of the fragmentary nature of the content and the failure of the survivor to provide either a coherent history or a sufficient context to the events recounted.

Oftentimes, the child had to ask about the parents' Holocaust experiences in order to receive any information. Other discoveries occurred indirectly. A child came across a memento of a parent's past. She overheard a conversation between mother and father or between friends of the family who shared Holocaust tribulations with her parents. Unable to confront the issue directly, a parent may have proffered a book and encouraged the child to read it. "This is my life." It is clear that some survivors wanted their children to know at least selective elements of their Holocaust nightmare.

> "I know a lot about their experiences, and have since early childhood. My parents were always very open and frank about their years in the camps. Stories were told in great detail—to each other, to us kids sometimes, to their friends. No matter who the conversations were between, I was always allowed to listen. I heard about the routines in the various camps they were in, about the especially cruel Nazis working in them, about harrowing escapes from death, about the terrible conditions, about the people they knew and loved who died. These stories were part of the 'folklore' of my growing up years."

> "I can't remember the first time that I heard about the Holocaust. I have always known about it and always knew stories about my parents' experiences and details about the deaths of many members of my family. My parents were in a DP [displaced-persons] camp in Turkheim, Germany, after the war and many of the people they knew there emigrated to the United States at about the time they did, so our house was often filled with these other survivors, and talk around the kitchen table was always loud and pained and angry about the war and the camps and the people who never made it. There were poker games I remember on Saturday nights that were always filled with survivors and their children and we all, from our first days, were fed stories of the camps. I think I was eighteen before I discovered that there were Jews who hadn't been in a concentration camp."

> "I know about my father and his family's experiences in the Holocaust. Since I was young, maybe six or seven years old, I had been

> told stories. My father made me aware of the Holocaust in order
> that our people never forget. He believes that if it isn't told, no one
> will believe or worse yet—remember. Every time my dad tells me
> the stories, he cries and chokes, but he insists on telling them."

Many of the children of survivors commented that there was a
continuous undercurrent of references to the Holocaust, particularly
triggered by a survivor's anger or sadness. "How I wish I had a
mother" or "You have no idea what I have already gone through." This
undercurrent was often nonverbal as well. One clinician writes: "I
remember an enraged young man accusing his mother of 'constantly
talking about it,' upon which his tortured-looking mother remarked
that she almost never talks about her past memories, if for no other
reason than it greatly distresses her. It was obvious that this boy took
his mother's look in place of verbalization. Indeed her appearance told
more than words could express."[1]

Clearly, many survivors did not wish to talk of their Holocaust
years, although this may not have necessarily been the case immediately after their immigration. While some survivors received material support or jobs from American relatives or Jewish relief organizations, they did not receive the emotional response to which they were
entitled. Listeners avoided the topic of the Holocaust and rationalized
their avoidance by thinking, "I don't want to stir painful memories."
The authors of *Generations of the Holocaust* stated, "Survivors learned to
be silent and to avoid evoking anxiety and guilt in others in order to be
accepted by them into a foreign humane society."[2]

Primo Levi unconsciously forecast the nonsurvivor's reaction: "Almost all survivors, orally or in their written memoirs remember a
dream which frequently recurred during the nights of imprisonment,
varied in its detail but uniform in its substance: they had returned
home and with passion and relief were describing their past suffer-
ings, addressing themselves to a loved one, and were not believed,
indeed were not even listened to. In the most typical (and cruelest)
form, the interlocutor turned and left in silence."[3] Refraining from
talking about their Holocaust years easily became habitual for survivors. The pain of rejection, the perceived disinterest, and the desire
for acceptance quickly extinguished the impulse to report. The lessons
learned from these early encounters in the New World were sometimes applied within their own families as their children grew.

But the survivor's reticence was determined by other factors as well. He may have anticipated an accusatory inquisitor ("How *did* you survive?") who would prick his ambivalence about outlasting the others. Reliving those times might prompt memories and images that could elicit survivor guilt. He may have feared the indictment of exaggeration. He may also have felt at a loss to describe the destruction accurately and fully. Levi asked, "Have we—we who have returned—been able to understand and make others understand our experience? What we commonly mean by 'understand' coincides with 'simplify.' "[4]

If the survivor dwelt on his near-death experiences, past anxieties resulting from his precarious hold in this world might be excavated. Surviving entailed a numbness to the death of others, a focus on one's own existence, and a denial of the odds against life. Feelings were kept underground, as they continue to be for so many.

Survivors' disinclination to relate experiences to their children reflected a desire to avoid imposing an unnecessary burden or inflicting unwarranted pain. Survivors, above all, wished to foster a normal family life once again. And while some children of survivors actively sought information from their parents, others indicated (usually nonverbally) that reminders of their parents' Holocaust past were simply too painful to admit. Accordingly, survivors accepted the cues of their children and closed the door on any discussion of their Holocaust experiences even when the child, at a later age, might have been better equipped to hear them.

For many survivors, talking about their Holocaust period revived a sadness or anger that threatened to overwhelm. One clinician has reported that the survivors who psychologically lost the most were often the ones least likely to talk with their children about the past.[5] I have observed that survivors who believed they suffered less than their mates or friends were often reluctant to recount their adversities as well. They felt relatively fortunate and willingly deferred any opportunity for sympathy. ("I was only in a labor camp. She was in Auschwitz. I didn't go through anything compared to her.")

Those survivors who did refer to their past a great deal tended to repeat the same stories. They seemed to have mastered their feelings concerning those particular events and willingly related them to their children. One participant remarked, "I have a feeling that the vignettes they have told me are things they are most comfortable with."

While parents may have frequently mentioned the deprivation they experienced, those disclosures were often made with the intention of exerting control over their children or eliciting sympathy from them or both. Thus, there was the comparison of the "plenty of now" with the "scarcity of then" and the implicit demand for greater appreciation on the part of the child. There was also an implied request: "Listen to me and do as I say so that I will not suffer more than I already have."

While sporadically referring to previous deprivation, there were subjects of which survivors rarely spoke. They did not speak of the personal torture, abuse, or humiliations they may have experienced. They did not wish to relive the pain or shame, and they wanted to avoid frightening their children with their vulnerability.

Survivors were also reluctant to stir the too-painful memory of a murdered spouse or child and any guilt associated with that loss. To have acknowledged those taken from them might have precipitated fears for their present children and the concomitant feelings of powerlessness to protect them. To talk of a previous child or spouse might additionally have implied, albeit irrationally, a question of one's total devotion or loyalty to the present family. The quality of "secretiveness" a few children of survivors used to describe the atmosphere in their home while growing up can often be traced to this issue. The artist Marlene understood this only as a young adult. "We heard stories our whole lives. I don't ever remember not hearing stories about the Holocaust. But there were always secrets. I was eighteen before I found out my father was previously married and had a daughter."

At first, Celia was angry. Later she empathized with her parents' reluctance to disinter their buried past.

> I thought I knew a lot about their experiences. But only recently, I found out my father had a family before the war. They kept it a secret from me. I found out from my cousin who casually mentioned it in passing. He assumed I knew. When I asked my father why he didn't tell me, he said my mother didn't want to think about it and out of respect for her he didn't tell us. It was very shocking for me to find out he had a wife and son. My mother tells me that the last few years he talks about his lost son a lot. The older my parents get, the more they talk about it. They want people to know about it before they die. . . . It's made me wonder what else they have kept from me. He walked around with guilt his entire life because of his inability to save his wife and child. When he talked about the Holocaust he always talked about his strength and his leadership qualities which he exhibited during his three years in Auschwitz.

Even for those survivors reluctant to talk about the Holocaust, some information eventually emerged. It may have been prompted by a single stimulus such as a television program or a news item. It might have been elicited by a child's naive question exposing a difference between a friend's family and her own. Information might also have been offered by a survivor to explain a self-acknowledged irrational act. Finally, those elements most difficult to speak of were often revealed during a developmental milestone or crisis in either the parent's or the child's life.

"An event in the news like the march in Skokie, or the 1967 war in Israel. Any time Jews were at risk might prompt some conversation about the Holocaust."

"My parents never talked to me about their experiences. Something on the television might trigger my mother talking. But it was always just a snippet. Food could do it. If something were thrown away, she would say, 'We never threw *anything* out.'"

"My parents never sat me down and said I want to tell you something so you will remember. Tidbits would simply drop whenever. A couple of stories were told when they felt they weren't going to live forever. I've sensed my father's discomfort when I've sat him down and tried to talk about it, although he finds it somewhat easier to talk about the Holocaust than my mother. My mother always says, 'Why are you asking these questions?' She's likely to get very upset. My mother is racked by guilt about having lost her daughter during the Holocaust."

"They would explain a certain shtick of theirs and where it came from in the war. For example, it is difficult for my mother to throw things out. She explained that when she was on the run all those years, every possession was so precious."

"A lot of stories revolved around sexuality. My mother and her friends talked a lot about their sexuality, how they were cheated out of their adolescence. Their physical development was retarded and their menstruation delayed for years because of their experiences in the camps. There was a lot of discussion of how screwed up their body image and sexual image was, how ignorant they were about sex when the war was over. I think they were jealous that I was having a normal puberty."

"Their experiences came out over many years. It was hidden from me but not actively. I would overhear them talking about experiences although I'm sure my parents knew I was nearby. They never spoke about the Holocaust while I was in the room. The facts didn't come out openly until eight years ago from my father. What precipitated it was my separation from my wife. At that time my father told me his wife and two-year-old son (who I am named after) were killed. Shortly after, my mother told me she had lost her first husband as well. They told me to console me and assure me that life would continue."

Many survivors did talk openly and explicitly about their experiences during the Holocaust. What motivated them to do so? For some survivors, the desire to bear witness was a crucial incentive to go on through their darkest and most difficult Holocaust ordeals. They felt a sense of loyalty to those who were destroyed and believed they would serve the function of gadfly to the conscience of the world in the postwar period. For a few survivors, educating the public remains their raison d'être. Even those survivors who did not speak openly of what they saw and experienced during the Holocaust urged their children, "Never forget that it happened."

We have often heard that Israel rose from the ashes of the Holocaust. The argument has been made that if Israel had existed during World War II, the destruction of the Jews would not have occurred. Until 1940 or even 1941 Jews might have emigrated from Europe and taken sanctuary in their own homeland. Indeed, Israel is presently seen as a bulwark against threats to Jews in any part of the world. Yet, even with the existence of a militarily capable Israel, most survivors still believe in the possibility of another attempted mass assault on the Jewish people.[6] (As some have said: "What the world learned from the Holocaust is that you *can* destroy millions of Jews and no one will care.") Survivors, therefore, often told children of their experiences in order to prepare them for a possible future onslaught from an enemy fueled by centuries of anti-Semitism.

Evidence suggests that survivors in Israel communicated more openly about their Holocaust past with their children than did their counterparts in the United States.[7] State-sponsored memorials and commemorations of the Holocaust became an integral part of the fabric of Israeli life soon after independence was achieved. This public recognition provided the needed emotional support for private discussions within survivor families. Fighting for and building a new Jewish state afforded survivors a sense of accomplishment and heroism to counterbalance their feelings of powerlessness during the Holocaust. Furthermore, those who immigrated to the United States as opposed to Palestine were more likely to focus their attention on assimilation and personal advancement as a further means of placing the Holocaust behind them. The survivor in Israel, on the other hand, was continually affirming his Jewish identity as he participated in the renaissance of a Jewish state.

"I think I know more about my father's experience because he took a very active role in saving himself. My mother felt she was just lucky," reported a participant in my study. Indeed it is often the case that survivors who were partisans during the war were the most likely to speak of those years and to engage in active discussion with their children. Those who fought and resisted were understandably less likely to be burdened with feelings of helplessness, shame, or guilt, which might have inhibited comment about their past.

There is variation not only in how much survivors related of their history to their children but also in the content areas or themes that were repeated. Some spoke mostly of an ideal pre-Holocaust world in which they lived, others related their subsequent experiences of persecution, loss, and deprivation.

Certain motifs were commonly depicted in survivors' recollections of Holocaust events: The continuous precariousness of life and the overwhelming element of luck in escaping death:

> "An execution was to take place because of an infraction of one of the prisoners in the camp. The men were lined up and every tenth one was chosen to be hanged. My father told me he was number nine."

> "What was communicated to me was that every day they didn't know what was going to happen to them."

When or how relatives died:

> "All I know about my father is that he saw his whole family shot in a ditch."

When or how survivors were separated from other family members:

> "All my father told me was that when his family arrived at the death camp, he was sent to the left and his parents and sisters to the right. He never saw them again."

> "My mother and grandmother were in the camp together. At one point my grandmother signed herself into the hospital. When my mother heard she ran to the hospital because she understood that was sure death. By the time she got there it was too late."

Acts of kindness, bravery, or heroism that survivors engaged in or witnessed:

> "My father was fortunate to get a job in the kitchen of the camp peeling potatoes. With those potato peels he was able to keep himself and two of his close friends alive."

> "My mother's friend got her a job as an interpreter in the camp and thereby saved her life."

> "When my father got off the train one of the Kapos whispered to him that he should say he was an electrician. Otherwise he would have been killed immediately."

> "The inmates were forced to watch a prisoner hang. Before they put the rope around his neck, he yelled, 'Long live the Jewish people.' My father told me that really strengthened himself and his friends."

Atrocities perpetrated on others that they witnessed:

> "My father hasn't spoken much but once he told me he saw young children taken by Germans and killed by smashing their heads against the wall."

How survivors manipulated the environment in order to survive and how they saved themselves or another at the last minute:

> "My mother had been at Auschwitz for a while when her sister arrived there. Her sister had already been selected for death but

> my mother bribed her way out of that line. How much hair you
> had indicated how long you had been at Auschwitz, so my mother
> surreptitiously got her sister's hair cut in order to save her life."

How survivors escaped incarceration or survived while hiding and
singular events that made an indelible impression on them:

> "My father told me a story of a rabbi in the camp who was
> throwing bodies onto a burning pyre. Earlier in the day my father
> had smuggled a potato to the rabbi. After the rabbi threw the last
> body, he cooked the potato in the fire of the heap of bodies."

Beginning at an early age, a child of survivors might question his
parents about the Holocaust. While many parents responded to the
inquiries (albeit carefully selecting various events while omitting others), some clearly indicated their unwillingness to do so.

> "My mother does not want to talk about it *at all*. When I ask her
> questions, she says, 'I don't think so. I just don't remember.' My
> mother gets very distressed even when other survivors talk about
> the Holocaust."

> "I found out about their Holocaust experiences because I asked.
> They never voluntarily brought up the topic. [They spoke of their
> experiences] only in response to my questions, . . . and even then
> not always."

Nearly half the people I interviewed acknowledged that they knew
nothing or very little about their parents' Holocaust experiences.
While this result can be partially attributed to the survivor's reticence,
some of their children were aware of choosing not to probe. They
feared inflicting further pain on their parents. They were apprehen-
sive of their ability to cope with their own feelings of fear, guilt, or
rage, which might be exacerbated by clear revelations as opposed to
the vague reference or intimations already heard and observed.

Some children would ask other survivors about the Holocaust while
continuing to refrain from directly approaching their own parents. By
assuming a similarity of survivor experience these children could satisfy a need to know about their parents while avoiding the prospect of

seeing their parents suffer further anguish because they would be asked to relive their past. And, by once removing themselves from their own family, they could also more easily quell the fear of their own powerlessness in the face of such adversity. ("If that could happen to my *parents,* what could happen to me?")

Many of the second generation exhibited a need to identify with their parents' suffering in order to understand more fully and to feel closer to them. Understandably, however, questions designed to satisfy these needs often had to await the mastery of unpleasant feelings associated with their parents' past experience and present behavior. Thus, children of survivors often refrained from approaching their parents for information until adulthood, when their fears and anger were more effectively controlled.

"My mother is very reticent to talk. She was hidden in a farmhouse of Gentiles outside of Vilna for six months. She minimizes the threats to her life and I never heard details of her experiences. I think, for her, the Holocaust was more difficult than it was for my father, and she desperately wants to put it behind her. She would never give you an interview like this. I sense this and I don't push it. I don't have a right to stir anything up for her."

"I didn't ask my mother questions. Hearing all those things would have only made me feel more guilty if I acted like a brat, so I just didn't want to know. I also wouldn't want to picture my mother like that."

"I was afraid to ask my father about his Holocaust experiences. At the dinner table I was a bad eater. He would say, 'If you only knew what I had to eat.' I didn't want to ask because I had these awful thoughts of him eating rodents or something."

"Until I was in my early twenties I assumed it would be too painful for [my mother] if I asked about her Holocaust experiences. She didn't offer any information because she didn't want to hurt me. But, at one point, we sat down and talked about our assumptions of each other. Even then she told me that if I wanted to know anything, it must always come at my request. As interested as I am about the Holocaust, I have never read a book, fiction or nonfiction, about it even though my feelings are very strong about Nazism. My mother's testimony was recently recorded and it took me months before I would look at it, and even then I only looked at part of it."

A minority of survivors talked of their Holocaust years with their young children. For various reasons, however, many more opened that door later. A keener sense of mortality impelled them to discussion. With greater distance from the Holocaust, their exposed nerves recovered their myelin sheath. Having adapted to and prospered in a new environment, their energies could be more safely directed to recollection. And, many decades after the destruction, the world seemed more willing to listen. Some parents have accompanied their children to Holocaust museums and traveled with them to international gatherings of survivor families. And they have talked. What are the effects of these disclosures?

For some in the second generation, being a child of survivors has become a central part of their identity. Hearing about their parents' experiences has perhaps enhanced feelings of closeness to them, and it may also have provided a sense of historical continuity if parents spoke of their prewar family life as well. Unfortunately, when the Holocaust is often referred to, the Jewish legacy implicitly communicated is one characterized primarily by victimization.

Children of survivors have reacted in a great diversity of ways to the disclosures of their parents. One clinician believed that the more the parent divulged of his or her Holocaust experiences, the more likely the child would become depressed and feel guilty about his relative good fortune.[8] Children may also feel guilty because of an irrational belief that either they were responsible for their parents' suffering during the war or that they have failed to compensate their parents for their losses.[9] (One woman I interviewed recounted a frequent daydream. She would be walking on a busy street near her home or riding on a bus when she would find her grandfather and bring him home to her mother, who missed him so much.) Attempting to stave off guilt, some children have reacted with anger and annoyance at their parents' information.

Investigators have reported that communication from parents about their Holocaust experiences affected daughters more adversely—making them more depressed, anxious, and withdrawn—than sons. A higher level of nonverbal transmission of Holocaust experiences by parents and an awareness of that background at an early age by children produced higher educational attainment by sons but greater psychological difficulties for daughters.[10] These gender differences may be a result of mothers having transmitted feelings of victimization in their accounts, while fathers were more likely to present themselves heroically, as one who had fought back, taken risks, and overcome his foe. Daughters identified with their mother and the role of victim. Sons were more likely to emulate their father, act "tough" and aggressively.[11]

Some children of survivors remember only heroic or triumphant aspects of their parents' experiences. Frequently, survivors elected to emphasize those deeds. It is not uncommon for children of survivors to perceive their parents to be heroes. Knowing of their parents' success in repeated life-threatening situations may also engender a feeling of invulnerability to future danger.[12] On the other hand, those survivors who ascribed their escape from death to luck may contribute to a child's sense of fragility, as the gift of survival is not only randomly bestowed but also reliant on factors not under one's control. In later life, the child's need for control may, therefore, become overdetermined.

Children of survivors may react to their parents' revelations with a myriad of feelings—anger, guilt, horror, sadness, pride, and so on, depending on, in part, the content and style of the disclosure. And despite the fact that survivors were prone to repeat the same stories over the years, their children often have difficulty remembering the details or sorting out the chronology of events. They apparently assimilated only selective elements of the stories. Their anxiety may also interfere with an ability to recall.

> "For a long time I kept forgetting details and needed to keep asking them to refresh my memory. Also, for a long time, I deliberately didn't want to know anything. In my home there was constant talk about the Holocaust and there was a great deal of hysterical rehashing of the events, which bothered me a great deal."

> "When I was about twenty-five or twenty-six my father told me that his child, S., was killed in the Holocaust. Only years later when my psychotherapist pointed it out to me did I realize that my name was the same as my murdered brother."

Ironically, it was often the older child of survivors who found it emotionally difficult to hear a parent's narrative. For younger ones the story was not unlike the tales he or she had heard read from books. It was an unreal world. As they neared adulthood, however, they could more clearly imagine the danger and horrors of the scenes described. Still, for many children of survivors, images they conjured up from their parents' stories were clearly imprinted even at a young age.

"In the fourth grade I remember standing with my mother in the kitchen while she was cooking and telling me Holocaust stories in a matter-of-fact way. It all seemed so normal. I was so young that I didn't really appreciate what I was being told. This didn't really happen to her and it also didn't impact me."

"I was always told stories. I would picture them. The imagery was indelible, for example my mother hiding in a haystack and the Germans using pitchforks to find her. I was terrified when I heard the stories and I don't think I could ever forget them."

Children's reactions frequently reflected their parents' emotions that accompanied Holocaust-related material.

"My mother was very protective of us. She didn't even want us to see the movie *Exodus*. References to the Holocaust were sometimes made—an uncle or grandparent who was killed. It might come up in conversation at the table on Jewish holidays. Bits and pieces came out—taking camp uniforms off dead bodies and wearing them, my mother being very ill with scarlet fever in the camp, eating moldy bread. My mother would walk away whenever anything came on the television, like films of the Nuremberg trials. When she did talk about it, it was with no emotion. For me it was a story. It could have been anyone else. I took my cue from her. It was only when I got older that it got harder for me to look at pictures or films."

"For me the Holocaust has always simply been a romantic fantasy. All my parents ever told me was that they met and fell in love in a concentration camp."

"I don't know that much about their experiences. I didn't want to ask when I was growing up because every time it was talked about my mother would cry. My father, the denier, would always tell stories humorously—how a Nazi put a gun to his head and pulled the trigger, but the gun was empty."

Whether survivors refrained from speaking to their children about their past or released scattered information over the years in short bursts, most of those in the second generation have wide gaps in their knowledge of their parents' experiences. Fantasies of their parents' Holocaust life and experiences, therefore, frequently emerged. Many children of survivors "have created a myth about the Holocaust or their parents' Holocaust experiences based on their own fantasies, particularly in families where parents had been silent about their personal experiences."[13]

Hannah, a twenty-seven-year-old business consultant, related the following: "Because I don't know much about my parents' experiences I used to have frequent nightmares about them. For example, in one recurring dream, the Germans were making soap and lampshades out of human flesh. My father walked on a selection line being inspected to see if he would be subjected to that. I only learned later in life that my father never went through any selections."

Such inventions often influenced children's perception of the survivor parents and, as a consequence, may have affected their attempts to cope with their parents' Holocaust background. For example, those who imagined their parents to have been meek and passive may have felt ashamed or angry with them. In addition, their own feelings of vulnerability may have been exaggerated. By contrast, children who perceived their parents to have taken an active or even heroic stand were not only more likely to respect them more but were also more apt to feel confident in the face of adversity.

Perhaps the most common concern of children of survivors, and one that fueled the most dreaded vision of a parent's ordeal, was the actions or behaviors the parent may have performed in order to escape death.[14] The answer to this question often played a central role in determining the child's view of that parent. Frequently, it was the child's imagination that produced the explanation.

One afternoon I received a call from a prospective patient. She was a child of survivors and had heard that I was as well. She first needed to reassure herself of this fact, however. Then she exposed the issue that perhaps troubled her most.

> "I heard you are a child of survivors. Is that true?"
> "Yes, it is."
> "Do you know how your parents survived?"

"Yes, I believe I do."

"Tell me how they survived."

"We can talk about that when you come in, if you would like."

"I must know now."

"Why is that so important to you?"

"I can't come in unless you promise to tell me. I know what my mother had to do to survive."

It became clear that this woman felt soiled by her mother's behavior and needed to know if I had also been "tainted" by my parents' experiences.

Many children of survivors I interviewed were concerned not only with their parents' past suffering but their present pain as well. When the parent does not voice a direct relationship between Holocaust trauma and postwar ongoing affliction, the child may feel an unwarranted responsibility for that distress. And because it is often the survivor who suffered the most extensive losses during the Holocaust who chooses to remain silent about those years, her child, thereby, has even more latitude with which to spin fantasies of the parent's past and ongoing victimization.[15]

Some of the participants described their homes as being permeated by an atmosphere of secrecy as they were growing up. The survivor who failed to speak of the events that affected him most in his life—those that occurred during the Holocaust—may have shown a more general lack of spontaneity as well in an effort to avoid the revelations or emotions associated with past trauma. He had to conceal who he really was.

Survivors vary greatly in their openness about their Holocaust experiences. While some remain silent, others lecture publicly to any group that will listen. Individual survivors may also purposefully select to whom they wish to disclose past experiences. Just as some children of survivors chose to seek out more information from their parents and remain close to the Holocaust while others fled what they perceived to be an environment stifled by those events, parents may have communicated their suffering to one of their children more than another. On many occasions an interviewee would spontaneously remark: "You should speak with my brother. He was told a lot more than I was," or "My sister has very different perceptions or feelings because she was much more involved with my parents' Holocaust." In most references, the oldest sibling seemed to be the most knowledgeable and to have been affected to a greater extent by the parents' continuing distress. One child of survivors, the youngest of three siblings, remarked: "It's weird to answer these questions because I never think of anything about myself being affected by the Holocaust." I never heard this absolution from firstborn children.

Those in the second generation thus vary widely in their general familiarity with the history of the Holocaust. One investigator reported that children of survivors do not have more factual knowledge about the Holocaust than their Jewish-American peers from nonsurvivor homes.[16] My observations confirm this finding. When a participant remarked, "I *feel* like I know a lot about the Holocaust and my parents' experiences, but after being asked questions I guess I really don't," he reflected a pattern I noticed in many others as well. These children believe they know about the Holocaust simply because they have perceived its aftereffects on their parents.

Similarly, many Holocaust survivors know little of the general history of the Third Reich and its program for the Jews. If you asked survivors what occurred at the Wannsee Conference, many would not know the answer. Some survivors have a clear understanding of the persecution of Jews that took place in their own country but not in others. In recent conversation with one survivor, I mentioned a book concerning the Holocaust that I highly recommended. It was clear that she had been offended in some manner. "I *lived* it. I don't need to read books or see movies about it." For this survivor, her experience was sufficient. She had personal, intimate knowledge of the Holocaust. All else, for her, was commentary.

The survivor feels pressures to remember *and* to forget. He has partial control over some of these influences and none over others. He strikes a balance between living in the past and embracing the present.

Most children of survivors were admonished "to remember." Their parent implored: "We must never forget that it happened. And we must not forget that it could happen again." But *what* must the second generation not forget? The answer to this question lies in books, films, and parental accounts. Yet, many in the second generation do not avail themselves of any of these sources. Six million is not an impressive number. It is abstract and it numbs rather than sensitizes. *One* person's story has the potential for illumination.

Children Describe
Their Parents

"They weren't your happy, normal parents. They tried very hard to live as normal a life as possible and enjoy it."

"My parents always gave anonymous charitable gifts. They didn't want to stand out."

It is impossible for us to see our parents objectively. Our own needs and the frustrations and gratifications experienced in the relationship color our perception. Nevertheless, that perception determines, to a significant degree, how we choose to interact with our parents. Our impressions of them also create expectations of the world which mirror our inferences about how that sphere has treated our parents. (Is the world a cruel or a safe place?) Ultimately, our perception of our parents moves us to emulate or distance ourselves from their character. And we nervously await the feared inevitability of our repetition of their dysfunctional features.

Many reports have indicated that composites of survivors presented by their children are disturbed ones. Survivors have been described by their offspring as emotionally unstable, agitated, mistrustful of others, obsessed (with food, cleanliness, money), and uninterested in life apart from work or family.[1] Compared with their Jewish peers who did not have a Holocaust background, children of survivors have described their parents as more depressed, fearful, suspicious, and withdrawn. One report indicated that children of survivors, in contrast to their peers, were also excessively concerned with their parents' physical well-being, despite, at times, recognizing that their vigilance was unwarranted. This same report indicated that children of survivors focused more on their mother's than their father's psychological and physical status. While these children were generally more protective of their parents than their American Jewish peers, their shield was extended to their mother to a greater degree that it was to their father.[2]

Why were these children more distressed about their mother than father? The mother was usually the primary caretaker during their formative years, and children of survivors thus experienced a greater need for their mother than for their father. Therefore, the stakes were higher when considering the well-being of a mother versus a father. It is understandable that children would have been more attuned to and fearful of any signs of maternal as opposed to paternal disintegration.

In general, contact between children and the survivor father was sparse. One researcher reported that while children of survivors did not describe greater closeness to their mother than their American Jewish peers with nonsurvivor parents, they did feel significantly more distant from their father and experienced greater discomfort in relating to him.[3] Survivor fathers worked long, arduous hours outside of the home, trying to succeed in their new country. Kept out of sight by their taxing work schedule, survivor fathers did not provide the continuous, vivid reminders to their children of their underlying fragility. In addition, children may have inferred strength and emotional health from their father's ability to work at such a strenuous pace.

Many immigrant groups have displayed a grittiness and industriousness in their attempts to realize the golden dreams of their new country. For most of these newcomers, having arrived with very little, the exigencies of the moment required that resolve. Holocaust experiences may have fueled a father's additional needs to protect and provide security for his present family. Feeling relatively powerless during the war, the survivor could finally assert control over his life and his environment. Hard work, accomplishing, may have been a significant source of renewed potency. For some fathers, *doing* was an *opportunity* to avoid feeling. Indeed, one study indicates that the degree of a father's traumatization during the Holocaust is inversely related to the emotional closeness and involvement of the survivor with his son.[4] The more deeply etched the emotional scars, the less he is able to tolerate an emotional connection to his male child.

Some investigators have reported that children of survivors were likely to perceive their parents as belonging to one of two categories. The children in one group idealized their fathers and mothers, focusing on assumed heroic qualities, qualities of mastery, strength, resilience, and adaptation. Those in another group, however, centered their attention on images of shame and degradation involving their parents, acts of humiliation in which their parents may have participated.[5] This latter emphasis, of course, resulted in an ambivalent response at best, and an extremely critical one at worst. Children need to idealize their parents so that they can be assured of a parent's ability to protect and foster their physical and psychological growth, and so that they can strive to be the positive models that their parents represent. The second group of children may not have had this need fulfilled.

I did not find the extent of idealization and devaluation of survivor parents by their children that has been reported elsewhere. (But neither did I find the degree of psychological problems in children of survivors noted in other accounts, and perhaps these two issues are related. To the extent that one's needs are excessive, one's perceptions of significant others will be distorted.) Perhaps these qualities were lacking because the respondents in my study were older than those participants in previous research, who were usually adolescents or young adults. As children separate more completely, both physically and psychologically, from their parents, as they increasingly seek fulfillment of their needs outside the family, they have greater opportunity to see their parents in a more realistic light. As they mature, they are less likely to view people as either one way or the other and more apt to understand the complexity of personality and motivation. They become more reticent to adore or condemn.

One researcher reported evidence indicating that, as children of Holocaust survivors became older, they came to view the Holocaust legacy and their parents more positively. With age, they were more likely to recognize the inherent strengths of their parents and perceive them to be positive role models. There was a "shift from guilt and shame to pride and appreciation . . . an increasing recognition and admiration for parents' attributes which enabled them to survive. . . . The dominant response describes parents as being resourceful, having common sense and practicality, and being incredibly strong. . . . Many participants feel that their parents' durability, resourcefulness, strong-will, determination, ambition and fight have been transmitted to them, enhancing their own ability to survive and overcome."[6]

Because children's perceptions of parents affect their own self-image, those children of survivors who felt special may have been more likely to view their parents admirably. On the other hand, those who primarily viewed their survivor parent as a victim may have felt diminished by their background.[7]

As individuals age there is often a tendency to develop a pride in their roots and thus search for information regarding their background. Reports of children of survivors in their thirties and forties are more likely than previous descriptions by younger offspring to demonstrate a valuing of their family's European history. Feeling different from one's peers is perhaps most disconcerting during adolescence.

> My background was a stigma for me as a teenager. I wanted to be like everyone else. I conformed in order to be accepted by others but I could not make my parents like my friends' parents who were contemporary, sophisticated, and less invested in their children. My parents spoke a foreign language which was a source of humiliation for me in front of my friends as it accented their 'differentness.' They were open about having been in concentration camps whereas I wanted to avoid any reference to it. It seemed to me that having been in concentration camps marked them as inferior people. It was difficult as a teenager to imagine my parents having been incarcerated for simply being Jewish. Therefore, it follows in my fantasy that the incarceration did indeed mean they were not as good as other people.[8]

There are additional reasons for the likelihood of a more positive perception of their parents by older children of Holocaust survivors. Until recent years, many survivors were reluctant to offer and many of their children avoided asking for information about experiences during the Holocaust. With more knowledge and greater comprehension of that period, children of survivors have an enhanced ability to empathize, to project themselves into difficulties their parents endured both during and after the Holocaust. And, of course, this empathy often contributes to reducing the anger the child feels over perceived deprivations resulting from impaired parental functioning. Furthermore, those of the second generation who have children of their own appreciate the formidable task of raising offspring even under the best of circumstances. This, too, may, therefore, diminish criticism for perceived injustices incurred at the hands of one's survivor parents twenty years ago.

In response to the question "In what ways (if any) do you perceive your survivor parent(s) to be abnormal as a result of their experience?" some participants repeated those characteristics associated with child rearing that have been previously discussed. Parents were overly protective, excessively involved in their child's life, and unable to recognize or accept the notion that their child was not as happy as they wished him or her to be.

A few children of survivors described a potpourri of symptoms, many of them reminiscent of those comprising the "survivor syndrome." As they spoke, I could often hear their anger and frustration (despite an awareness of the origin of these symptoms) at having parents so debilitated, so unable to provide the quality of parenting to which they believed they were naturally entitled. Marsha became increasingly agitated as she recited a list of her father's deficiencies. "My father is guilt-laden, depressed, overly dependent, easily aroused to intense rage, very manipulative, unable to listen to others, unable to see others as individuals." Doreen reported:

> They are both very high-strung, very nervous, very easily upset and aggravated. They have both had various stress-induced illnesses and physical ailments. Although the two of them are quite different from each other in personality and behavior, they each have a whole assortment of neuroses. One has a real martyr complex and takes on the role of a victim in almost every relationship and doesn't know how to be assertive enough; this one suffers silently, doesn't sleep well or eat well, and knows how to induce guilt. The other one has an enormous ego, is usually insensitive to everyone else's needs, loves to tell long self-glorifying tales, and has an unpredictable and violent temper. These two are as mismatched as a couple can be, and they've spent years torturing each other—and those close to them. I have to conclude that the terrible years they lived through during the war made them far more neurotic than they would have been if they had led a peaceful, normal life.

As Doreen ended her description, the resentment in her voice had been replaced by a profound sadness.

Scenes from childhood illustrated Steve's perception of his parents.

> My father is a very stubborn man. He keeps his own counsel and is unbending. He is "abnormal" in his stubbornness yet it is very much a strength of his as well. He once bought some sapling willow trees and planted them in our yard. Unfortunately, a hurricane hit a couple of days

later and would have blown those saplings away except that Dad spent the entire night outside in the storm, holding onto the willows like Samson chained to pillars of stone. I remembered we looked out the window and my mother said, "That man is not normal." She was right.

But she wasn't much better. I think she had built up inside herself a tremendous self-hatred because of her survival. The commandant at Buchenwald would praise my mother for the good work she did and years later, when she talked about his praise, she would flush with pride and then almost immediately would panic from her shame. She could never stand praise. If someone told her she was pretty or sang well or anything it would make her very uncomfortable and very sad and she would tell us about how pretty her sister had been or how beautifully her mother sang. She devoted herself to her children and got all her pleasure from them and also her pain.

An interesting thing about her—she was twelve when she went into the camp and seventeen when she got out—there were no other survivors from her family and she couldn't remember when her birthday was. That memory had been lost in the camp. She knew that she had been born in the spring but other than that had no idea exactly when. I'm not a psychologist, but I bet that most twelve year olds who are separated from their relatives and from written records would still be able to remember their birthday. I'd bet that could be considered an abnormality caused by the Holocaust.

My mother was a strong woman but she didn't perceive herself that way. She panicked easily and we learned early that if there was bad news she wouldn't want to hear it. She was hysterical and emotional and would go off uncontrollably at almost anything. It was my birthday once and I wanted a party and wanted to have friends over and the whole scene, but because we didn't have enough money we were going to have just a little celebration with just the family instead. My mother baked a cake and started to sing "Happy Birthday," and I told her it was the worst birthday I had ever had. She panicked, got hysterical, started screaming and smashing the birthday cake all over the floor. I was astonished by how large her emotional response was.

She took a group of kids swimming to the lake once, and when we were driving home there was a roadblock set up by the New Jersey State Police. My mother had forgotten her wallet and didn't have her driver's license with her, so she made us children lie down in the back of the car on the floor and put a blanket over us while she talked her way through the roadblock.

I have to stress that while my parents were abnormal, it wasn't necessarily all bad. It was powerful and zestful. It was never indifferent. There was passionate involvement and commitment in every area of our lives—although perhaps just a bit out of proportion.

My father was stubborn, angry, violent, uncompromising, irrational, and extravagant. He was also isolated, sullen, and completely uncommunicative. But he is untiring, committed, and thoroughly honest as well. My mother was hysterical and emotionally needy. She was also giving, loving, and brave. These abnormalities were clearly from the Holocaust. No one ever doubted that fact or questioned it in our household.

When discussing their own problems, the predominant theme of many children of survivors, particularly the females, was fear. It is not surprising, therefore, that the most frequently mentioned perceived parental abnormality was an apprehensiveness observed primarily in their mother.

"My mother is mistrustful in general. She is very anxious, very fearful, and phobic. She is afraid of losing her children, her family. She is in constant fear of losing her life. She has a very difficult time making decisions and choices. She agonizes over their ramifications."

"My mother is excessively afraid—of physical dangers such as earthquakes, robbers, and so on. She is also excessively cheap, possibly as a result of her losses during the Holocaust."

"My mother's self-esteem is extremely low. She fears people in uniforms (even is intimidated by mail carriers), bolts when she hears German accents, has intense nightmares, is inordinately fearful about the future (hoards money and food). My father, although quite successful in the business world, is extremely hypochondriacal."

"They are afraid of any officials such as police, the IRS. They are secretive. They don't trust others and are often very calculating. They are also very emotional and overly reactive."

"My mother is very tense, prone to anxiety. She worries excessively. She has certain habits; for example, she still takes rolls from restaurants—this is the last-meal mentality. She may be too close to her children. There's a kind of hovering. I don't think she'll ever be *truly* happy because she'll always turn around, remember, and see what happened. I don't think we could ever give her enough in terms of personal achievements that would make it go away. She might overreact to a particular stress or loss and I know it's not just this but also because of what happened. That's why we won't tell her anything bad. You can't have a realistic relationship with her. Bad news has to be diluted enough before we would tell her about it. She can deal with *death* very well and be strong. She must have seen so much of it and that must be why."

Not surprisingly, male survivors were more likely to express their anger directly than their female counterparts. While a few children of survivors described periodic outpourings of rage, even more reported a caldron of tension that continually simmered, ready to boil over at real or imagined affronts. Most survivors were able to control their anger and present a mask of conviviality for public consumption. For others, however, the facade collapsed in the safe confines of their home.

"I think that my father lives with too much guilt and hate that eats him alive everyday."

"My father was always tense. There were so many things that would trigger his anger—war movies, anything having to do with Germany or Nazis. The world was clearly still a potentially dangerous place to him. He had little patience with others, including his children. He was quick to judge. Punishment of his children was physical at times. He didn't speak about it, but you knew what he was so angry about—his family, which was completely obliterated during the Holocaust."

"My father is paranoid that his life is about to end. He is almost two-faced. He is wonderful with friends, a real joker. With his family, he flies off the handle at the slightest provocation. You have to walk on eggshells with him."

A prevalent manifestation of anger evidenced in survivors is their mistrust of the world. For most survivors, presumptions of human goodness were dashed by the events of the Final Solution, as well as by their personal experiences during that period. Germany, the most civilized nation on earth, failed them. The gentile world failed them. God failed them. Friends failed them. ("My parents' personalities are extreme. If they do something, it's one hundred percent. They live by black-and-white principles. If a close friend disappoints them even once, they cannot forgive.") And, perhaps, unconsciously, they felt parents failed them as well because of their inability to shield or protect.

These beliefs sometimes resulted in a partial withdrawal from human relationships and a constricted focus inward to the self, to immediate relatives, and to the Jewish people. "My father doesn't trust *anyone* outside of his *immediate* family. They both just cling to their children to the exclusion of any other social contacts. *Everything* in life revolves around the question Is it good or bad for the Jews?" This emphasis is abetted by an enhanced sense of preciousness and precariousness of a family member's existence. In addition, the excessive control they exerted on their environment, their impulses, and their children may have been anxious attempts to quiet previous feelings of powerlessness.

Survivors waited, expecting future disappointment. At times, their high standards served to fulfill this prophecy as others were placed on probation while inevitable trial and error ensued. Cynicism was thereby continually reinforced. "For my mother, everyone is the enemy until they prove differently."

For severely depressed survivors, a preoccupation with anger and experienced losses diminished their ability to empathize and help with the problems of their children. Now, as they age, some survivors find themselves increasingly despondent, perhaps because of the reduction of physical and psychological resources which, heretofore, had been sufficient to cope with their past travails.

The partner of a depressed survivor may have functioned well at the outset of the marriage but later succumbed to the strain of living surrounded by such despondency. Just as disconsolate survivors were unable to extend themselves to their children, they were incapable of providing nurturance to their spouses. A joyless marriage takes its toll. Furthermore, such survivors may have been a constant reflection of the despair which their mates attempted to bury. Prolonged exposure to this mirror sometimes subtly promoted the excavation of those interred feelings.

> "I don't find them happy. I'm not sure if that's Holocaust related. I think they just went on living without any zest for life. It [the Holocaust] must have had an effect on them. My mother's youth was cut off. My father is a very guarded, nontrusting person, and my mother is depressed. When we didn't listen as children, she would break down and cry and say how hard life has been for her. 'You don't know how hard a life I've had growing up without parents.'"

"I think my parents are addicted to their pain. They are locked into the past."

"My father is deeply disturbed by his past. He constantly refers to the loss of his first family. He has been in a state of depression for the last ten years. His health has been poor since I can remember. He has recently become obsessively religious and superstitious. He has tremendous rage toward the Germans. My mother is extremely energetic, full of life, an optimist—at least much of the time. More and more, as she gets older, she's been subject to periods of depression and a certain hopelessness."

While the previously described survivors exhibit pervasive, debilitating emotional responses, others manifest a paucity of feelings. To have allowed themselves the awareness or expression of emotions during that period of darkness might have proven disastrous. In many instances, survivors had to numb themselves in order to proceed effectively. After liberation, some survivors continued to divorce themselves from their feelings because of a fear of further vulnerability to loss, a fierce desire to move away from the pain of the past in order to live a "normal" life, and/or a dread of being overwhelmed by sadness, anger, and despair. Several children of survivors described an expressive deficit in their parents.

These parental limitations were evident to Joshua, a thirty-year-old businessman. "My mother has never been the typical Jewish mother. I don't remember her cooking much, worrying about how I would get dressed. She's not very nurturing as a mother. My mother didn't express much feeling. She did have a *terrible* temper, which she would infrequently express. My mother seems to lack interest in developing close relationships especially with men. She divorced my father after a bad thirteen-year marriage. Dad had a hard time showing affection and relating to his kids. It's because of his preoccupation with the events of the past."

While Susan, the painter, respectfully acknowledged the "tough," "resilient" side of her mother, she also spoke of her parent's shortcomings. "My mother lacks emotion—or perhaps she simply doesn't display it. She never cries. It is rare to see her laugh. She recently was surprised on her birthday with a new car. She had no reaction. It's as if she's worried it will be taken away from her if she shows any happiness."

"I feel that my father has developed some abnormal character traits as a result of his Holocaust experience," Joshua remarked in a matter-of-fact manner. "He is unable to express emotion in any way. He never becomes very excited, enthusiastic, or emotional about anything. Also, he does not express disappointment or sadness. My father almost always has the same sense of demeanor, whether things are going well or not. My father also has a distorted view of earning, saving, and spending money. He believes that one should work hard and save because a disaster, illness, or problem may occur at any time. . . . My father has shown very little encouragement and reinforcement for the achievements and success of his children. He has not been overly critical of our decisions, but he also has not shown much of an interest."

In addition to describing their parents' emotional difficulties, a few respondents noted health problems of their fathers that had their origin in Holocaust experiences. Finally, several children reiterated that, from their vantage point, the most evident parental abnormality was an overinvolvement and excessive psychological investment of the survivor in his or her child's life. "They can't cope with their children being anything less than extremely happy and successful!" one participant exclaimed. Another remarked, "They are abnormally devoted to and involved with their children."

Only a few participants reported no abnormalities in their parents as a result of the Holocaust. They inferred an absence of psychological disability, at least in part, I believe, from the appearance of both material and social success achieved by their parents and many other survivors.

> "Until this interview I hadn't thought about how the Holocaust had affected my father—partly because he seemed so intent on getting on with his life."
>
> "I've never considered my parents to be abnormal. I've always considered them as very strong because of how they coped during the Holocaust and were successful after the Holocaust."

While some children of survivors simply stated that they found it too painful to acknowledge any abnormal aspects in their parents, many of them had low expectations of their parents; if these were met, normal functioning was implied. ("After what they've been through, what do you expect?") These children adapted to continuous moderate levels of anxiety or irritability in their parents, and these emotions were then seen as within the "normal" range: "That's simply the way survivors *are*." As Karen, a thirty-four-year-old advertising executive, noted: "I didn't know what an easygoing house was like until I spent extensive time in my college roommate's house with her parents. Everything wasn't an issue. Voices weren't always raised. There weren't automatic reactions blowing things out of proportion. Even though there was a lot of love in that home, people just let each other be. It was a revelation for me, another way to live."

Survivors made commitments after the Holocaust—to remember, to bear witness, to remain vigilant against its repetition. For many, however, a powerful motivating force was a desire to make up for lost time, to put the Holocaust behind them, to proclaim their survival and vitality despite Herculean efforts aimed at squashing them, to live as fully as possible. As one man remarked of his parents, "They have incredible optimism, zeal for living. They have a sense of obligation and duty to help others even if they don't like them. Every day they talk about how lucky they are." And yet, even in this glowing description, the last sentence may indicate a certain ongoing uncertainty. "Every day they talk about how lucky they are." Perhaps they feel their luck might expire at any moment.

In many households children of survivors grew up observing not only scarred parents but also a marriage in which the survivor couple were of disparate intellectual or social standing, what one clinician has termed a "parental disequilibrium."[9] In their urgency to leave the past, avoid loneliness, obtain a protector to calm their fears, and begin a new life, many survivors chose mates precipitously. Love, physical attraction, shared interests and values were criteria often overshadowed by a need to feel understood, a desire for safety, a wish to feel connected to one's prewar setting and family. In many cases, loving feelings developed over the years via shared future tribulations and positive bonding experiences such as the birth and rearing of children. Apparently, in almost all cases, as time went by, a mutual dependency and protectiveness that brought these individuals together deepened and, thereby, solidified the relationship. It is unusual for a marriage of two survivors to have ended in divorce.

The offspring of these mismatches were affected in various ways as their observations were oftentimes reinforced by explicit verbalizations of a parent. "I never would have married him if not for Hitler." The exceptional, and perhaps unnatural, origin of one's family was underscored.

Understandably, such mismatches often spawned ongoing marital displeasure and frustration and, hence, another reason for a shift of focus to the children. This transfer of attention may have led to the overinvolvement, overprotectiveness, and overinvestment in a child's life which has been repeatedly described by many children of survivors. In families where one spouse perceived the other to be inordinately traumatized by the Holocaust and, therefore, too fragile to be assaulted with dissatisfaction, a mismatch of partners may have also resulted in the displacement of anger onto a child.[10]

Understanding the contrariety of their parents' marriage and the extraordinary circumstances that allowed it to happen may produce many different responses in children of survivors: "I want to do well in order to compensate for my mother's/father's disappointments, both past and present." "I want to do well in order to distract my mother/father from her/his disappointments." And, perhaps, felt most unconsciously, "I wouldn't be here if it were not for Hitler." It is possible that a consequence of this notion might be guilt, as well as an inordinate desire to please in order to counterbalance the costs (the destruction of the Holocaust) which enabled one to come into being.

Almost three-quarters of the people I interviewed came from two-survivor families. One-fourth of this group described an unhappy marriage between their parents, while noting many of the factors that contributed to parental disequilibrium.

> "My parents married because they both found themselves in a refugee camp in Germany after the war and they were alone and lonely. Both regretted the marriage but stayed married because of the children. There has not been much love between them— there's been companionship and dependency on one another. Mostly, my mother has been taking care of my dad because of his illnesses."

> "Their relationship is not a good one. They are close but there's a lot of bickering and dissatisfaction in my father because of my mother's behavior. She won't travel, she won't be away from her children, she is fearful of everything, she doesn't like to socialize. As my mother's anxieties became intensified in later years, their relationship has deteriorated further as my father becomes more helpless."

"From the beginning it was a terrible mismatch of personalities. They had survived the Holocaust. Their families had both lived in the same city in Poland before the war. But this was about all they had in common. My mother was reared in an upper-middle-class, intellectually oriented, sophisticated home. My father's family lived 'on the other side of the tracks.' My mother's first husband, the great love of her life, was killed during the war. The marriage of my father and mother was, for the most part, a loveless one."

Sheilah, the mother of two quoted earlier, told me:

My parents are two completely different types of people who have never really understood each other and have been battling for almost fifty years. My dad is a strong-willed, physically and mentally active person. He is quite self-centered, very full of himself, his good deeds, accomplishments, and his own feelings. He carries male chauvinism to the extreme—my mother is not allowed to express an opinion about business, politics, what gift to buy someone, home repairs, anything. He has a terrible temper and can fly off the handle for any reason, becoming verbally abusive and sometimes violent to the point of throwing things and threatening physical harm (though never quite going that far). He can also be very impulsive and irritable, driving everyone around him crazy by his sudden shift of moods or change of decisions.

My mom is the quiet suffering type. She perceives herself to be a victim of a bad marriage, which in many ways is true, I guess, since I think she would have been a much happier person with a calm, accepting husband. She can't stand not being allowed to express an opinion on any important subject. If she does say something, she gets screamed at and sometimes not spoken to for days. She is almost constantly hurt by something or other that my father has done or not done and nurses her hurt feelings quietly, usually telling only me or her best friend. She can, however, be annoyingly martyrlike sometimes. She also has a certain controlling side to her nature, needing to tell her loved ones what to do, what to wear, what to buy, when to come and go.

These two people are so intelligent, so basically sweet, that it's a shame they had to marry each other. They would have both been better matched with other types: my dad with a stronger more assertive woman who wouldn't take abuse and bossing around, my mom with a gentle, quiet man who wouldn't push her around and would appreciate her more.

Since I can remember, they fight endlessly. They bicker, they quarrel, they have screaming fights, they slam doors, they sleep apart, they don't speak for days. Unfortunately, they have used me and my brother and friends as referees sometimes when things were at their worst.

About one-third of the participants portrayed their parents' mismatched relationship as having "worked," at least in some aspects. It may have been a marriage which began for the wrong reasons but matured into a stable, even satisfying one. Many of these unions were strife ridden but nevertheless gratified intense dependency needs. In some of these relationships, differences and dissatisfactions between spouses were masked in the years following liberation by the external stresses of establishing themselves in a new country, only to emerge more clearly later in life when the family's physical security was ensured.

> "It's an excellent marriage. They're both very strong and stubborn. My dad left child rearing entirely to my mother and his role was breadwinner. They love each other a lot. When they first got married, they weren't in love. They got married to form a nest and establish a connection. My mother told me that, when she got married, she wasn't sure it would work. After their first child, they built a life together. They respect each other a lot. They depend upon the other. They're each other's best friend."

> "I don't think they would have gotten together if not for the Holocaust. My father's background was much more affluent than my mother's. They are very good friends but there is nothing romantic between them. Only recently have I heard them say they love each other. They're such different people. My father loved my mother from the beginning. My mother married my father because he was a good person. They were always working, doing, accomplishing. They never took vacations. They have never been affectionate. They are *inseparable*. If something happened to one, the other would be totally lost."

> "My father seemed like the king of the universe. Everything was done not to make him angry. My mother totally obeyed him. He was physically in bad shape so she took care of him a lot. He loves her a lot and is very protective of her. He says she gave him the will to live after the Holocaust. He also gave her a lot of strength after the Holocaust. He was significantly older than her and well off when they met. She was the girl who married the older guy who has taken care of her."

Steve, the actor, described his parents' marriage:

Their relationship was a stormy one. They fought often but they were quite devoted to each other. I always felt that their loyalty to each other was in the nature of an obligation to their lost family members. This was particularly true for my mother. I think my father loved my mother more right from the beginning of their relationship, although he wasn't very demonstrative about it. On my mother's side, however, it was clearly duty. She complained about him bitterly all the time I was growing up and was threatening to divorce him from when I was a child until shortly before her death. It's odd but I don't think she ever mentioned the divorce to him, only to us children. We often wondered why she just didn't go and do it. I rarely remember her being affectionate with him but can often remember him getting playful and sexual with her. She would be annoyed by that sort of behavior as if it were coarse and inappropriate.

I think there might have been a bit of class conflict between them. My parents were second cousins but my mother always stressed that their families were very different. My father came from a family of "prosteh yidden (uncouth Jews)," who weren't well educated or religious. They dealt in horses and were rural. My mother's family, however, boasted of a rabbi and an author and even one sister who had been involved in Yiddish theater. Neither of my parents had been educated but my mother might have felt that she married beneath herself. My father didn't even have a beard before the war and I've heard my mother say that he dressed like a goy. Her family, on the other hand, had been very pious. They were "shineh yidden (nice Jews)."

A lot of their problems revolved around us children. She would take our side in things and that would cause conflict and fights between the two of them. My father, for a long time, resented the children for that and truly felt that we came between him and her love. For her part, we were a buffer zone between her and him and I guess she used us as a way to avoid him.

Michael, the accountant, had this to say:

My parents are second cousins. My father had had a crush on my mother since childhood. My mother had never liked him. After the war, a surviving aunt paired off the few surviving nieces and nephews, including my parents. My mother said that when they married she did not love him, but that she had tremendous respect and trust for him. I remember her jokingly staving off affection from him when I was young. I also remember plenty of bickering. They have a lot of fun together *socially*. Their marriage is neither great nor horrible.

Among the parents of the people I interviewed, about a third of the marriages between a survivor and nonsurvivor ended in divorce, an unusually high figure for marriages involving Holocaust survivors. In some cases, the pair were raised in very different environments (Europe and America) with their concomitant different frames of reference. After stating that his parents were divorced, one child of survivors explained: "My father is a typical eastern European, far different from my mother's American upbringing. They are so different, it is hard to believe they got married in the first place." Postwar circumstances may have incited their misguided decisions, and again, those who waited several years before marrying may have chosen more compatible partners.

More important, perhaps, adding to this discordant background was the essential feeling of most survivors, "Anyone who wasn't there could not know what it was like. Consequently, anyone who wasn't there could not possibly understand me." And, just as many survivors trivialized the difficulties felt by their children, they also lacked empathy and/or sympathy for the problems of their mates. "You think that's a problem? Go through what I went through and you will know what real problems are." For some survivors, this superiority of suffering justified their preoccupation with themselves to the detriment of their sensitivity to others. Ultimately, some of the survivor's symptomatic traits—such as a need for control, hyperirritability, mistrust of others—arising from the Holocaust trauma may have proven, for the nonsurvivor, too difficult to live with over an extended period of time.

Sarah, a thirty-five-year-old school principal, witnessed a marriage that seemed doomed from its outset.

> My parents were married thirteen miserable years. Dad escaped from camp, ended up in New York after the war. He loved another woman, who married his friend, since Dad couldn't provide for her. My mom [a nonsurvivor] loved another man her parents didn't approve of, and with her parents' push married Dad, ten years her senior. Her family had money and helped Dad get a business started. There were several fights—verbal and physical, police involvement, and so on—before they finally split. Dad is a loner. He tried one other marriage twenty years later that ended in annulment. He is a perfectionist and is comfortable being alone. My mom would probably say Dad's experiences contributed to their downfall. Who knows?

Some survivors married nonsurvivors by chance—being at a certain place, at a certain time, and coming into contact with someone whom they found attractive, compelling. For many, however, their choice of one who had not been traumatized also reflected an attempt to start life over again, to escape reminders of one's past, to envelop oneself in a "normal" other, and in some cases, to feed off that other's strength. Reports of the outcome of many of these partnerships were very positive indeed.

> "They have a wonderful relationship. They know each other well and are *very* tolerant of each other. My mother [the survivor] and father are very close. I can't picture one without the other. They are inseparable."

> "I believe that my mother chose a nonsurvivor spouse in order to provide a balance for her children. I see this as a positive response to her deficits. My parents have an excellent relationship—rocky at times—but whose relationship with your partner is not rocky at times? My dad told me that he chose my mother because she had qualities which he did not feel he had to give his children. My mother is certain that my dad embodied the best of what a person could be. He is warm, brilliant, sensitive, caring, loving, compassionate, and so much more. My mother has the drive to succeed, is very giving and passionate about life. They saw in each other the best of what they wanted for themselves—and for their children."

> "They are very happy and fulfilled. They have a great time together. My dad is my mother's husband, boyfriend, lover, and father. He is the big protector and he takes care of my mother. She likes that. She finds a lot of security in her marriage because he would never allow *that* to happen to her again."

The experience of similar trauma often produces a particularly powerful affinity between individuals. They are more likely to feel truly understood, to experience greater empathy for the other, and to feel a responsibility for the emotional protection of the other. All these aspects hold the potential for a close, committed relationship. For survivors, these factors, as well as a common European background with its attendant perspectives, may have compensated for any "parental disequilibrium." In addition, survivors usually had some confluence of postliberation goals—to rebuild a family, to have as normal a life as possible. Of the participants in this study whose parents were both survivors approximately half described the marriage which they grew up observing in positive terms.

> "Their marriage is wonderful. They were very in sync with each other. They never didn't speak to each other. They always helped

and supported one another. They loved to be together, even if it was just eating an apple on the couch watching the news. They were inseparable. They didn't go out much."

"My folks had a good relationship. My mother was the affective, emotional component, my father the more intellectual, theoretical type. Both could be highly sentimental at times. My mother did not allow anger into the relationship because she feared it (the disapproval that she thought came with anger). My father, by contrast, did not allow anger for 'principled reasons'—'civilized people do not get angry.' But, generally, they had a very good, and close, and supportive relationship."

"I think of it as a traditional European marriage. The roles were very traditional, with my mother doing the housework for much of my childhood, until she went to work in a business with my father. Both parents were involved in all major family decisions, and I remember a pretty peaceful relationship, with the occasional argument. I remember a very strong bond, with no inclination (to my knowledge) toward separation 'to meet individual needs.' "

"My parents married in 1940. My mother was from a poor family, my father's was well-to-do. They eloped. It's been stormy and loving. My father understood early that my mother did not come out of the Holocaust well. He protected her materially and emotionally from everything. They don't communicate much and find it impossible to talk about problems. They don't talk about feelings. The prospect of people separating because they don't get along is unacceptable to them. I think they have a generally happy and productive marriage."

"They are a very strong *unit*. I know they love each other. We never saw them fight or be very affectionate with each other. I think they were very sexual but we didn't see it."

It is virtually impossible to assess confidently the effect on children of survivors of perceiving their mothers or fathers and their parents' marital relationships as dysfunctional. One can only note the person- alities of the children and the parents, the quality of their interpersonal relationships, and their approach to life and then hypothesize indirect links. (According to one clinician, children of survivors have particular difficulties with intimacy.[11] If so, is the problem a consequence of the quality of the parent-child relationship, the marital relationship of the parents as understood by the child, present societal factors making commitment and unselfishness more difficult to embrace, the child's extrafamilial experiences while growing up, or other factors? Do children of survivors have greater difficulty with intimacy than others of their generation who do not share a Holocaust background?) The *degree* of parental impairment (as well as those *particular* characteristics that are impaired) and marital dissatisfaction exhibited by the parents can also be important influences.

One further source of conflict in some marriages between survivors warrants mention. It surrounds the issue of remembering. Some survivors felt a deep obligation to "tell the stories," both for themselves and for others. Conversely, many survivors wished (just as fiercely) to avoid the intrusion of their past into their attempts at normalization. In a marriage with these divergent orientations, both partners may have experienced significant frustration and resentment.

Nevertheless, further testimony to the strengths of survivors is the high number, in this study, of survivor marriages perceived positively by their children. Despite having had dear ones murderously wrenched from them, survivors again allowed themselves to love, commit, and be vulnerable to another.

6

Jews and Gentiles

"You scratch a non-Jew and you find an anti-Semite."
"What Hitler couldn't do, intermarriage is doing."
—Holocaust survivors

Lessons. The world, I learned, is divided in two. There are Jews and there are goyim. There are few of us and many of them. Goyim are different from Jews. They are brutish. We are sensitive, humane. They persecute. We study. We must stick to our own, for community and safety. Goyim are to be shunned. They are to be feared. And because Jewish survival is, and has always been, precarious, we must focus our energies on ourselves, our families, and our people. We live in America, but we are Jewish and alien here. It's been like this for generations. We live in their countries and they hate us. And, sometimes, they decide to murder us.

I was eight years old when I visited a church for the first time. We were in Montreal, sightseeing, and this church was one of the oldest in North America. It was Catholic, cavernous, and dark. Hundreds of candles flickered from distinct corners, an eerie, foreboding, continuous incantation in their language of prayer sent shudders through me. Crosses everywhere I turned my head with him writhing and bleeding. I thought I might be snatched up or killed. I ran out, panicked.

A survivor returns to his village in Poland after liberation. It is evening. He approaches his family's house, peers in the window, and sees his former Polish neighbors eating around his dining-room table. He knocks on the door, fearfully. They recognize him and awkwardly extend an invitation to join them for something to eat. They are using his china, dishes which his parents ate from. He eats the soup that is offered. No one acknowledges anything, the past nor the present. He finishes his soup, rises from the table, thanks his hosts, and leaves. Ten meters down the street he turns his head to look for a final time, but only for a moment. His pace quickens and then he starts to run. *Loif, yid, loif.* Run, Jew, run. They can kill me even now.

Most survivors communicated their angry, suspicious attitude toward the gentile world to their children.[1] For it was not simply the Germans, Poles, Lithuanians, Ukrainians, and other nationalities who participated in the Final Solution. More to the point, it was the goyim. This critical stance taken by survivors was continually reinforced, for, in many cases, children of survivors grew up surrounded by Jews with similar attitudes.

Children of survivors reacted to these lessons about the gentile world with a range of responses. Some exclusively retained the particularistic concerns of the Jewish people; others demonstrated their enhanced empathy for the oppression of Jew and non-Jew alike.[2] One team of investigators reported that, compared with their American Jewish peers of nonsurvivor households, children of survivors demonstrated more altruism and compassion for other malevolently treated groups.[3] A handful, in their rebellion against the myopic, ethnocentric view of their parents, focused only on the disadvantaged outside of the Jewish fold. They asserted that Jews, today, were safe, secure, and derived a significant degree of power by their assimilation into the Establishment. Perhaps this perception and the turning of their attention outward also served to quell any underlying apprehensiveness concerning the questionable foundation of that security.

Given the history of the persecution of the Jewish people and the exclamation point of the Holocaust, one might wonder why more survivors did not shun their Jewish legacy and attempt a more thorough merger with the majority population. Yet, it was the rare survivor who denied his Jewish identity, refused to circumcise his son, or completely embraced the gentile world.

"How has your family's Holocaust background affected your attitude toward non-Jews?" I asked the people I interviewed. Not surprisingly, a few echoed the theme of philosophers for whom the Holocaust brought, once again, into stark relief, questions concerning the nature of man, and pessimistic conclusions of his predilections. "When I see goodness in others," one said, "if a gentile stranger goes out of his way to help me, I'm amazed that there are good people. I believe too many people have a propensity to evil and violence."

While only a few of my respondents reported having been directly, personally, confronted with anti-Semitic slurs, many others, nonetheless, indicated a deep-seated mistrust of non-Jews. These qualms did not simply mimic their parents' verbalized suspicions, nor were they only a result of their family's Holocaust background. They reflected a particular reading of the long history of Jewish-Gentile relationships. For some children of survivors, the endurance of the Jews, despite unrelenting persecution, has imbued them with a sense of superiority as they identify with their resilient, death-defying people.

> "I'm very much on guard with non-Jews, particularly about the smallest anti-Jewish or anti-Israel comment. I'm probably not even objective about this sensitivity. Growing up in a Communist country [Rumania] made me on guard with everyone. I believe that if the great majority of non-Jews had it their way, they would do away with us in two minutes."

> "Whatever my attitude is toward non-Jews is a result of the Holocaust and the persecution of Jews through the centuries. If I don't trust non-Jews it's because of the Jewish experience, not simply my mother's. In general, I'm a skeptic when it comes to people. With non-Jews, I'm even more skeptical. When it comes right down to it, no one cares about Jews but Jews themselves. Biblical literature tells us that God told us the Gentiles won't like us, so I believe Him."

> "You can't trust non-Jews. Jews aren't in power. Goys don't like Jews. Things don't change. The Jew stands alone. There is a basic undeniable mistrust toward non-Jews. There is a decided rapport between two Jews and lack thereof between a Jew and a Gentile. I always knew there was no way I could ever bring home a non-Jewish boyfriend, let alone marry one. No way! 'Shiksas bring shkutzim [a derogatory term for gentile men]' was a direct quote of my mother when I was growing up, and all hell broke loose when my sister went to a homecoming dance with a Gentile in high school."

> "Their background has had a *tremendous* effect. It has caused me to be defensive, not open, to feel different. I believe all non-Jews have a little streak of anti-Semitism in them. Through high school

and college, my friends were Jewish. Non-Jewish acquaintances I made along the way, I haven't kept up with. Now that I have a family, I have less contact with non-Jewish friends. I don't think I could have as close a relationship with those outside of the tribe."

"I grew up in Wisconsin. There was always a bit of suspicion. They are the enemy. But because both of my parents were involved in the university, there were always non-Jews in the house from all over the world. You always knew the good goyim from the bad goyim. The flip side is that any group that is singled out I have a certain sympathy and understanding for. But I sometimes feel like I can't worry about *them* because I have to worry about me."

"I was taught not to trust non-Jews, that when it comes right down to it, when you're really in a bind, non-Jews won't be there for you. That, in tough times, they would turn you in for a loaf of bread. Growing up, I believed people in non-Jewish homes had a 'lighter' time and there was some attraction to that. I don't feel at home with non-Jews and I have an unsettling doubt—that if IT happened again, they wouldn't be there for me."

A few participants described a much more benign view of non-Jews. Their own oppressed background served to sensitize them to ethnocentrism and discrimination and enhanced their compassion for the plight of the other. In two cases, this more favorable stance toward the non-Jewish world was also related to the relative lack of Jewish identity of their parents and/or to growing up in the midst of a mostly non-Jewish world that did not make them feel different.

"Because of what Jews went through as far as discrimination, I went out of my way to make sure I didn't discriminate. It always baffled me that my parents would have prejudices after what they went through. My parents communicated that you should stick with Jewish people."

"If the Holocaust has affected me at all, it is in terms of a greater acceptance of all people. I can't discriminate against another group just because they're different."

"My parents always wanted to know what religion my friends were but it was always okay to be with non-Jews. My parents were very assimilated German Jews. They still put up a Christmas tree every year."

> "It hasn't affected my attitude toward non-Jews. My parents always said you can't trust the goyim. They turned Jews in. But it didn't rub off on me."

Several children of survivors longed for the normality of the dominant stream and an identification with the unscarred. A rebelliousness against the Holocaust legacy and burden of suspiciousness and hatred was expressed. A few of those I interviewed described an almost counterphobic attraction to Gentiles. Perhaps this lure indicated their desire to assert that the world *was* a safe place for Jews, that Jews were not in peril from "them."

> "I believe it is easier to be a non-Jew in this world. I am sure that is the truth. I have always thought that it was more fun to be a non-Jew, and that non-Jews were less analytical and less self-obsessed people. In short, they are happier people. As a young man, I sought out the company of non-Jews because I felt that I would be happier around them, and yet I am and have always been more comfortable with Jews. . . . I always sensed that my parents were distrustful of the gentile world and I think I reacted in the opposite way. I made a point of being around them, almost to the exclusion of being around Jews and of trusting and confiding and being very personal and intimate with them. Despite my closeness, however, I do not expect Gentiles to be capable of understanding the Jewish experience."

> "It's made me rebel against my parents' paranoid attitudes that the entire world hates the Jews. I went out with a lot of non-Jewish men. I always had a liberal attitude about minorities. I think I became more sympathetic toward non-Jews."

> "It probably made me seek the companionship of non-Jews—mostly men—not at all associated with the Holocaust. I would feel some peace in the conversation. I find myself overreacting when I hear racist comments by Jewish people. I get very upset. I hate it when Jews speak about or infer their superiority. Part of that may be because my husband is not Jewish."

> "I date almost only non-Jewish women. I've always been more attracted to non-Jewish women because of the dissimilarity from my overly protective, overwhelming mother, and to continue the assimilation process. I'm bothered by the stereotype of the little Jewish kid, the ghetto kid."

When I asked my respondents, "Would you marry a non-Jew?" seven (15 percent) replied affirmatively. This figure was significantly less than recent reports indicating a 30–40 percent rate of intermarriage among the general Jewish population of North America today. It must be emphasized that, for the great majority of my respondents, the reluctance to intermarry did not derive from an adherence to Jewish law. (Only a small fraction of them could have been characterized as religiously observant Jews, as measured by their response to my question "Approximately how many non-holiday Sabbaths a year do you attend synagogue?" Very few attended Sabbath services more than six times a year.) Rather, the low number reflected the fact that the core of their Jewish identity sprang from their relationship to the Holocaust, and not from their adherence to Jewish statutes or their knowledge, for example, of Jewish history or Jewish literature.

Other reports have consistently indicated that children of survivors display a greater motivation for cultural continuity than their American Jewish peers, even those who are second-generation immigrants but do not share a Holocaust background. For American Jews whose parents were not involved in the Holocaust, intermarriage poses the threat of the dilution of Jewish culture, but "for survivor children, haunted by their parents' recollections of death and near death, intermarriage consciously or unconsciously represents a threat to cultural survival."[4]

Children of survivors appear to be more resistant to cultural assimilation than their American Jewish peers,[5] and one investigator, Axel Russell, has gone so far as to suggest that they isolate themselves from non-Jews in order to avoid the impoverishment of their cultural heritage.[6] My interviews did not confirm this last-mentioned finding. Many children of survivors do have gentile friends. Those who choose to associate almost exclusively with other Jews do so as a result of their deep-rooted mistrust of Gentiles, the comfort they derive from being among "their own," or the perceived similarity of values and interests.

For children of survivors, ensuring cultural continuity may serve the function of reiterating the existence of their parents and themselves. In a recent conversation with a member of the second generation living in Germany, I asked him how he felt, as a Jew, growing up there. "I *like* being here. Every time I meet a German who knows I'm Jewish, it's like saying, 'I'm here. You didn't get us all!' "

Many of those I interviewed voiced a particular sensitivity and obligation to perpetuate the Jewish people. For some, it was a felt responsibility to those who had been murdered in the Holocaust (as well as to those who preceded them) to keep their tradition, their soul, alive. In an age when many are eschewing parenthood, children of survivors have experienced a poignant need to propagate and instill their offspring with a Jewish identity. On a practical level, their refusal to marry a non-Jew implies a recognition of the importance of shared values and customs in producing a commonality of purpose and direction to their marriage.

> "I was dating a non-Jew for three years, but I realized I couldn't marry him. Judaism was too important to me to give up. I wouldn't give up my tradition. There are certain feelings and values you grow up with that you want to share in a marriage that I wouldn't be able to share."

> "I dated non-Jewish women when I was younger although I was aware you weren't supposed to do that. Today I don't date non-Jewish women anymore. The biggest tragedy one could do would be to intermarry. The thing my parents always threw in my face was, 'To marry a non-Jew would make the suffering of the victims of the Holocaust in vain.' I had a *responsibility* to only be involved with Jewish women."

> "I don't know if I would marry a non-Jew. I wouldn't because of my relationship with my parents. But I can't picture myself meeting someone whose values were the same as mine and saying, 'I can't marry you because you're not Jewish.' I can't see having a family with a non-Jew. I have a responsibility to the Jewish race. I can feel my murdered grandparents hovering around me. I would just prefer marrying a Jew. It would make my life easier."

In their refusal to marry a non-Jew, several children of survivors simply acknowledged the importance of a common frame of reference. Others mentioned the desire to feel understood, which would be more likely with someone from a Jewish background. A few emphasized the need for their mate to comprehend their Holocaust consciousness.

> "I did not even consider marrying a non-Jew while I was single. I dated many non-Jews, but always knew that I would never marry and have a family with a non-Jew. . . . I wanted to marry a Jew

because I believe Jews share similar beliefs about life, family, success, humor, and priorities. I believe that my family would have been devastated if I had married a non-Jew."

"I absolutely would never have married a non-Jew. As it is, I'm happily married to a Jewish man. Even as a single person I always felt it was very important to marry in the faith—not only a Jew but one who felt *strongly* identified as such. Not only did I feel that the responsibility for Jewish continuity was on my shoulders and that of my Jewish peers, but I felt a mutual connectedness with other Jews which was lacking with non-Jews. Being with a goy would be like living with an alien. It would not have felt like home."

"I do not have as much in common with someone who is not Jewish, especially with regard to my parents. I just don't feel they would understand me and who I am. My parents' history is part of me and I think it takes an extraordinary person to understand— whether Jewish or Gentile—who does not come from a comparable place. But I believe a Jew would be more likely to understand."

"One reason I wouldn't want to marry a non-Jew is I feel she would never really understand me as a Jew and a child of survivors. If I wasn't a child of survivors, I could more easily marry a non-Jew, but there is so much feeling coming out of that history that my Jewish nonsurvivor friends don't even have. For me, to marry a non-Jew would almost be like being a *traitor* to what happened."

A reason often mentioned by respondents for not marrying out of the faith was a desire to avoid inflicting pain upon their parents. Indeed, most survivors view a child's intermarriage as a tragedy, a surrogate of Hitler's work, a betrayal of their own murdered parents' legacy to perpetuate the Jewish people. Their origins in eastern Europe, which was suffused with an Orthodox presence, and their rage at the non-Jewish world make it extremely difficult for survivors, even those not religiously observant, to accept converts to Judaism (particularly those converted by a Conservative or Reform rabbi) into their families. Two of those in my sample found themselves and converted spouse less than fully accepted by their parents.

"It would break my parents' heart. I couldn't even date non-Jews. For my parents' sake, I've never let myself think about this on my own. I just know this is *one* thing I'm not supposed to do."

"It would kill my parents. Being an Ashkenazi, I married a Sephardic Jew and that even feels different. So it would simply have seemed too uncomfortable for me."

"I wouldn't, not because of my own beliefs, but because I fear that my parents would reject me. And, if things got rough, my religion would be thrown in my face. I also wouldn't be willing to raise my children as non-Jews."

While mistrust of Gentiles is common among children of survivors, only one subject in my study, David, a thirty-year-old Orthodox businessman, clearly voiced this dynamic as primary in his refusal to consider intermarriage. "There are enough problems in marriage, you don't need another. Ten years into a marriage, she might turn around in the heat of an argument and say, 'You dirty Jew.'"

For many children of survivors, the search for identity that began in their teens and continued in their twenties, ended with a homecoming in their thirties and forties. Perhaps the trial-and-error process of the formative years of young adulthood finally brought a greater appreciation of what had been available all along. Perhaps the maturing process which moves the individual from a more narcissistic, present-oriented involvement to a greater recognition of community and historical perspective took hold. Perhaps the child of survivors made peace with his parents so that he could fully return to his close and extended family. Perhaps she learned more details of the Final Solution and her parents' harrowing escape from that grand design. Perhaps he contemplated the ramification of having children of his own.

A twenty-nine-year-old child of survivors wrote in response to one of my questions:

At an earlier age, I believe that many of my close friends were non-Jewish and non-white. But at age twelve or so, I realized that they were not true friends. I have become involved with mostly Jewish friends (many of them children of Holocaust survivors) since that time.

I was filled with anger and had many problems with the world at large since age fourteen until about twenty-three. When I was twenty-three I went to Lebanon during the war (August 1982). I came back confused and did a great deal of soul searching. I came to conclusions about my role in Jewish destiny and realized that I almost had to thrust myself into the middle of war to come to terms with my feelings about the Holocaust.

I realized that my long-time inability to trust others, relate to my own feelings, express myself in a meaningful way was directly linked to the confusion I had due to the experiences I had growing up in a family where so little attention was paid to the realities of my mother and grandmother during the war. I had to know what it was about so I could put it behind me. At this point in my life, I began studying the Holocaust feverishly.

Concerning the question of intermarriage, several children of survivors voiced a change in attitude as they grew older.

"When I was young and single, I enjoyed rebelling for rebelling's sake. I also didn't know myself very well until my mid-twenties. So I did once consider the possibility of marrying a non-Jew. Fortunately, I didn't. I realize now that it would have been a terrible mistake. Being Jewish and the traditions and feelings which that encompasses are so much a part of me. I can't imagine having a husband who didn't share that."

"I would marry a non-Jew. I have married a non-Jew. I have divorced a non-Jew. I think at one time, I preferred the idea of marrying a non-Jew but that is very different now. I would prefer to marry a Jewess and hope someday to find one whom I can tolerate and raise a Jewish family with. I know I am more attracted to the shiksas of this world, but, if I could choose, I would want to make nice for my parents. Why? you ask. Because my Jewish life and tradition have given me more and more strength as the years have gone by, and that is something I would want to give my children when and if I have any."

Several children of survivors indicated that they would marry a non-Jew. For three subjects, a non-Jew was clearly a preference, an endeavor to escape what was perceived to be an oppressive background, and/or an attempt to still fears of vulnerability to another genocidal assault. Yet, even those who would not shun intermarriage showed a sensitivity to cultural extinction. These respondents told themselves that Jewish tradition could and would be maintained in their new family, regardless of the religion of their spouse.

"I did marry a non-Jew. I was attracted to him because he had those qualities (even-tempered, never using guilt as a weapon, didn't try to control me) which made me comfortable. I had a real eating-disorder problem and when I was with him I had none. . . . Since I was sixteen I enjoyed dating people who weren't Jewish. Part of it was probably to drive my parents crazy. I may have also felt safer with a non-Jew. If ɪᴛ happened again, maybe they wouldn't get me if I was with someone who wasn't Jewish. . . . I married a non-Jew because I wasn't crazy around him. I was nineteen at the time and I wasn't conscious of all this. I didn't want to marry a non-Jew. It was that 'Jewish' evoked a certain craziness in me which made me unhappy."

"Yes, I probably would [marry a non-Jew] if I fell in love with a non-Jew. I do not feel that marrying a non-Jew would take away from my Jewishness (as long as he was not a *practicing* Catholic or Muslim). He'd also have to really have an interest in Jewish culture. He wouldn't necessarily have to convert but it would be important to me that my religion be dominant in the household and that my children be raised as Jews."

Other investigations have concluded that children of Holocaust survivors are more strongly identified Jews than their Jewish peers from an American background.[7] A history of familial persecution based solely on being defined a Jew, and a commitment to cultural permanence, certainly contribute to the greater psychological embrace of their ancestral ties. This intense affinity for their group may also lead to feelings of alienation from the larger culture in which they reside. Children of survivors frequently identify with and feel compassion toward other groups who have been discriminated against because they too are seen as being out of the mainstream, in a way not a part of the gentile world. Children of survivors may have fought for the rights of blacks during the civil rights movement because blacks were not perceived to be a part of the gentile majority, but a group marked for oppression by a gentile society, as Jews had been at other times and in other places.

Choosing a marital partner, for children of survivors, is a complicated matter. The decision involves consideration of one's ancestors, one's parents, and one's future children. But, what about friendships? Do children of survivors demonstrate the same general insularity as they do in their views of marriage? I asked my respondents, "Do you have more Jewish close friends than non-Jewish close friends? Is this at all related to the Holocaust?" Three-quarters replied that, yes, they had more Jewish than non-Jewish close friends; less than a quarter had about the same number of Jewish and non-Jewish close friends, and very few had more non-Jewish than Jewish close friends.

The majority of those who reported having more Jewish than non-Jewish close friends, however, did not believe this was due to their Holocaust background. Many grew up surrounded by other Jews. Some chose Jewish friends early in life, and those ties endured. (Most deep friendships do not develop in later life, but, rather, are cemented via shared experiences during our more formative years.) Many of my subjects reported an attraction to those who had similar values and customs and whose personal conflicts originated from the Jewish experience. These similarities would naturally engender a feeling of being understood, perhaps the most powerful ingredient in a psychologically intimate relationship.

> "I have always had more Jewish friends than non-Jewish friends. I don't think this has anything at all to do with the Holocaust. I don't particularly look for only Jewish friends. It's just that my husband and I seem to gravitate toward Jewish people more. Maybe we have more in common with them, shared sensibilities, a shared frame of reference, certain common understandings."

> "My close friends are those I grew up with—one from yeshiva, one from secular high school who was a child of survivors, one from college I met at Hillel. We share a common perception of the world, have similar concerns, anxieties, vulnerabilities, the need to procreate and pass on the basic important things to the next generation."

> "Most of my friends are Jewish. I feel that, with other Jews, you start at a different point of understanding, a different point of knowing each other."

Most groups tend to trust those who are members more than those who lie outside of the group, particularly if there is strong motivation for identification with one's group. For children of survivors, the group's centripetal force has been enhanced by its confrontation with death and extinction. Remaining among one's own also provides opportunities for the expression of anger toward those perceived enemies on the outside, and allows for the reinforcement of feelings of superiority in relation to others.

"I never feel comfortable with non-Jews. I always wanted to believe there was no difference—but there always was. I don't trust non-Jews. I think non-Jews always see you as a Jew first and not as a person."

"I have more Jewish close friends and it is related to the Holocaust. I want to be friends with those I have a commonality of interest, feel comfortable with. A certain insecurity has come out of the Holocaust for me. I feel a tension, almost a discomfort with non-Jews. There's a cloud over those relationships because of the Holocaust. I'm not always conscious of it, but it's there."

"I'm always attuned to what I sometimes perceive as anti-Semitism. Yet prejudice is a stupid thing. It is based on what people *think* and not on what they *know*. How can you truly hate that which you don't know or understand? A lot of anti-Semitic comments which I have overheard or been subjected to were based on not what someone *knew* but on what their parents or peers taught them. . . . It angers me when I hear non-Jews placing Jews into a stereotype. As ethnocentric as it seems, I think we [Jews] are generally more ethical, virtuous, intelligent, and refined than non-Jews. Of course, I would never share this with a non-Jew!"

During most of my childhood and adolescence I lived in a Jewish neighborhood in Brooklyn and attended a modern Orthodox synagogue. I knew that my friends and those I met at shul were Jewish, but they were clearly different. They didn't seem to be authentically Jewish, not *really* Jewish. They didn't come from homes where Yiddish was spoken. Their parents didn't have accents, further indicating that they did not come from the heartland of Judaism, eastern Europe. Real Jews were immigrants. These Jews were actually Americans. These Jews had nothing to do with the Holocaust. One other thing. They seemed so *relaxed*.

Some reports suggest that children of survivors feel a greater affinity toward immigrant Jews than second- or third-generation American Jews.[8] One study indicated that children of survivors not only limit their circle of friends to other Jews, but may further circumscribe their social world to include only other children of survivors.[9] I believe this latter observation proves more accurate for children of survivors when they were younger. As this group aged, they naturally came into contact with a wider range of individual backgrounds. They became, therefore, more desensitized to differences that may have, at first, seemed very foreign and, hence, presented obstacles to intimacy.

For Solomon, a thirty-seven-year-old dentist, American Jews seemed almost as foreign as Gentiles. His sense of responsibility for the continuity of the Jewish people also provoked his anger toward those Jews who were less committed. "My having more Jewish close friends is definitely related to the Holocaust. As soon as I know a person's religion, it immediately colors *all* aspects of my relationship with them. I've always felt more comfortable with those from a European background. I feel somewhat different and estranged from American Jews, who I perceive to be much more assimilated. I know there's no way to escape. They'll get you anyway, so why lose your sense of identity?"

Just as firstborn children of survivors sometimes bore the brunt of the compensatory desires of their parents to make up for what was lost, they were also likely to have lived a more insular Jewish life than their younger siblings. As survivors became more comfortable in their new environment, they were apt to venture forth into a wider world. Therefore, their later children may have been the beneficiaries of this greater exposure. It must be remembered that survivors' Holocaust experiences engendered an array of perceptions and responses to their new surroundings. On the one hand, some, despite their own lack of religious conviction, sent their children to yeshiva in order to protect, to ensure, a continuation of Jewish identity in a gentile country. At the other extreme is the survivor who chose to send his son to Catholic parochial school while attempting to hide his Jewish heritage for fear of renewed persecution.

Differences in worldview and orientation according to birth order were apparent in the family of Marty, himself the father of a son and daughter. "The majority of my close friends are Jewish. I do not believe this is related to the Holocaust, but I do believe it has to do with the upbringing of my close friends. All of my close friends share similar Jewish beliefs in family, caring, sharing, goal orientation, and success. My younger siblings do not have as many close friends who are Jewish. They also do not have the advanced education and degree that I possess, and they are less goal and success oriented. My siblings do not associate with many Jewish people, and, therefore, have fewer Jewish friends."

Finally, the Orthodox Jewish life style of two of my respondents hampered close personal contact with non-Jews. "My husband is Orthodox, so we find it easier to socialize with Jews about 75 percent of the time. This is mainly because of not going out Friday nights, not eating non-Kosher foods, and so on," replied Rochelle, a thirty-six-year-old psychotherapist.

For many children of survivors, being a Jew means belonging to a group that has been unrelentingly persecuted. Despite a strong Jewish identity, this consanguinity is primarily bound to the Holocaust, as these individuals often know relatively little of Jewish history, religion, or custom. One might expect, therefore, to find at least an ambivalent response to being born Jewish in a perennially hostile world.

Still, in response to my question "How do you feel about being Jewish?" the great majority of participants in my study reported a pride in the traditions, values, and resilience of this group with which they strongly identified. (I do not believe I would have heard the same enthusiasm and passion from their American counterparts who did not share a Holocaust family background, and who, for the most part, were assimilated and unconnected to the Jewish community.) Again, it must be emphasized that adherence to or knowledge of religious principles was not a salient element for most. The factor most frequently stated as generating this positive response was "tradition." Adherence to traditional customs and the use of the language (Yiddish) of recent past generations provided the psychological and spiritual link to murdered relatives whom they never knew but missed nonetheless.

> "I feel very good about being Jewish. I feel like I'm lucky to be a Jew. Even though so many terrible things have happened to us, we have a wonderful religion, tradition, and values. I feel connected to this wonderful history. It's something that links me to my grandparents and uncles whom I never met."

> "I love being Jewish. It's always been very important and central knowing the history of survival of the Jewish people. I take great pride in that. I have more trouble with assimilated Jews than non-Jews. As a child of survivors I feel a mission to keep Judaism alive."

> "I am happy and proud to be Jewish. I am proud of our history— such an ancient and dramatic past we have. I like the way we, as a

family, care for one another and reach out to others in the community. There's a sense of sharing and goodwill. I think my being Jewish has a lot to do with the compassion I feel for the downtrodden, the underdog, and my abhorrence of racism. For me, being Jewish includes a responsibility to seek justice. I really equate those feelings with being Jewish."

"Judaism is at the center of my self-understanding. I have dedicated my life to Jewish learning, Jewish action, and bringing others into the Jewish world. I have taught Sunday school and been a Jewish camp counselor. I have taken dozens of classes in a wide range of Jewish subjects. I work for the Jewish community and travel often to Israel. In so many ways, Judaism has been the central theme in my life. Most of my best experiences, serious growth, and self-awareness have sprung from the Jewish context. It is who I am."

"I'm proud to be Jewish even though I'm not a religious person. Judaism offers good values of how to live life. Now, with what's going on in Israel, it's more complicated. I felt being a Jew made me different, not better, just different from those I went to school and worked with. I've always felt Jews are a cut above intellectually and in other ways. I find American Jews different from European Jews. They seem a lot more assimilated. European Jews are more ethnic. I feel much closer to Jews with an accent. When I hear an accent, I feel like going up and chatting with them. European Jewry is me; really, eastern European Jewry. The prospect of them dying off is really sad to me."

For many of my respondents, being Jewish brought with it an important sense of community. Perhaps this indicates a huddling together in reaction to historical persecution. More likely, this community provides a substitute for grandparents and the extended family whom they never met. Marty told me:

The Holocaust is always at the back of my mind. It's all part of the burden of being a Jew. We've been persecuted for thousands of years. It's always more burdensome to be part of a minority. But there's also a sense of pride. I'm proud of being a child of survivors, that my father went through what he did and made it. . . . I feel good about being Jewish. I think it's a religion to be proud of because of its attitudes toward family, tradition, and customs. When a Jew meets a Jew there is something that holds them together, that they have in common. Be-

cause there are so few of us there is a feeling that you want to stick
together. . . . I feel like I'm part of a large family.

Several participants voiced more than pride. They described an
attitude of superiority in comparison with non-Jews. They often mentioned the resilience of the Jewish people, an extension of the very
positive identification they felt with their parents as survivors. Perhaps this feeling of superiority reflects the disadvantaged minority's
common perception of moral superiority to their oppressor. It may
also be symptomatic of a reaction formation to historical attempts
(particularly those of fifty years ago) to implant an inferiority complex
in the Jewish consciousness.

> "I feel very good about being Jewish. I've been given the tools
> through Judaism of the secret of survival which makes me supe-
> rior to the rest of the world. I have a sense of history which others
> don't have. I don't believe we are theologically the Chosen People,
> but our history has been so rich and ethical and has put us on a
> morally higher plane than others."

> "I like being Jewish. I'd rather be Jewish than something else. I like
> the heritage. There's something exciting about a close connection
> to the Holocaust. There's a specialness about that. There's a
> *uniqueness* about being Jewish in a way that other people don't
> have. I feel like there's a respect for Jewish people because of what
> they went through. When people, especially non-Jews, find out
> my parents are survivors, it has a real effect on them. I become the
> center of attention about that."

> "I make a differentiation between Jewish survivors and Jewish
> nonsurvivors. I always felt almost proud that my parents were
> survivors. Perhaps I thought they were better Jews because of all
> they had sacrificed and been through. I always felt I was better
> than other Jews. I felt proud, almost as if *I* was there."

Some children of survivors experienced their Jewishness, at least
partially, as a burden, especially when they were younger and their
awareness of being different increased their adolescent feelings of
insecurity. As children, they may also have harbored more negative
impressions of and resentment toward parents. For a few participants,
the disproving of negative Jewish images became their personal en-

cumbrance. I should point out that even though these individuals experienced the onus of Judaism, they rarely turned their back on that identity.

Joseph, the pediatrician, told me:

> It's a complicated thing being a Jew. It's an important part of my identity. I struggle to find ways to make it important to me and my family. I don't have any intense beliefs about a personal God, but peoplehood and community are very important to me. I support organizations like ADL [Anti-Defamation League], my synagogue, Jewish day schools. . . . It's made my life difficult. It's good and it's bad for me. It places a burden on me. I don't allow myself to do average things like go to a ballgame. Everything to me is serious. It's made my life serious. Other people are probably more interested in simpler things and are able to enjoy and be happy more than me. Being Jewish makes me think about prohibition, death, that we're a *minority*. It's burdensome. I feel like I've been entrusted with a heavy load to pass to the next generation. Like *The Book of Abraham*. I'm in that chain.

My old acquaintance Harry was more upbeat:

> I now feel very proud of being a Jew, and relish the depth of that experience. It is ancient, rich, tribal. I feel superior to the yuppie world and feel that the Jewish experience (the way I conceive it) is on a higher moral and spiritual level than the schnorrerdom of the rest of the world, particularly the glitzy, materialistic Protestant world. . . . When I was younger, however, I felt a lot of embarrassment and humiliation about my Jewishness. It made me feel out of place and weak and ineffectual. I don't really know how much of that is Jewishness or being a foreigner. There is a certain part of me that feels just a bit more vulnerable to the dangers of the world by being Jewish.

From Marsha, the pediatrician and mother of two, I heard a history marked by emotional change:

> From the first to eighth grade I went to yeshiva and I had a very strong Jewish feeling and Jewish pride. Suddenly, in the eighth grade, I *had* to get out of yeshiva, out of that religious element. Suddenly, the laws, the rabbis, didn't make sense. I've never gone back to that life. There are a few times when I miss not having a whole Jewish unit (my husband is not Jewish) such as on the High Holidays. . . . Everyone knows I'm Jewish and that's fine. There are also times I try to be Jewish in terms of

family values and social issues. Ten years ago I was much angrier at being Jewish. Both in yeshiva and at home I heard so many bad things about non-Jews—they were no good, you couldn't trust them. It made me crazy living in America like that. Leaving home, psychologically, I wanted to escape that paranoid attitude bombarding me with hatred.

More recently, I have become less angry, more comfortable. My mother's view is that people will always identify me first as a Jew, and I believe that. (She warned me that when my non-Jewish husband would get angry with me, he would call me a Jewish bitch. That's not happened. When my husband gets angry with me, he simply calls me bitch.) . . . I am proud that I'm a part of a people who has survived thousands of years of persecution. I am sad that so much of being Jewish is isolating, violent, and brings hatred upon it.

Leo, the television writer, was in some ways more positive:

I *love* being Jewish! I like being a Jew culturally. I'm not very religious. I'm superstitious enough to qualify as a Jew. I like having a Jewish soul. I think it gives me something special that non-Jews don't have. I like Jewish people. I like being with Jewish people.

I don't like being Jewish in a non-Jewish world because I feel I have to always prove that I'm not any of the stereotypes (for example, cheap, materialistic). There are certain Jewish things I really dislike—the gaudy Miami beach mentality, some of the pressures that go with being Jewish. For example, you have to be successful. You can't pump gas and be Jewish. I wish you could be Jewish without having to *prove* anything.

Some participants voiced clear resentment and even fear because of the vulnerability of Jews. Only a very small number, however, reacted primarily with these feelings—many fewer than one might have anticipated.

"I resent being Jewish at times, the religious aspects and constraints. I resent being a minority which is so hated. Because so much anger and hatred were heaped on my family during and after the war, it would have been so much easier being born a non-Jew."

"Sometimes, after thinking about all our people's suffering, I think, 'So what would have been the big deal of just being a Christian? Being Jewish was not worth the Holocaust.' I'm worried about anti-Semitism, that Jews are such a small minority in America. It makes me feel guilty that I brought my children from Israel to a goyish country."

"I feel neurotically nervous about being Jewish. I'm hypersensitive about people staring at us and harming us because my husband wears a kipa. The older I get, the more neurotic I become about the possibility of another Holocaust, so I'm more sensitive about anti-Semitic incidents."

It was highly unusual to find a respondent who did not have intense feelings associated with his or her Jewish identity, whose legacy as a member of this particular people did not arouse an impassioned response. Only one participant described a different point of view. "I don't think about being Jewish most of the time. It's not an issue, not a part of my identity. When religion is discussed, I tend not to mention I am Jewish, and I don't participate when the conversation turns to the Holocaust." This individual was raised in a highly assimilated home where a Christmas tree was routinely present during that holiday season. When asked if she would consider marrying a non-Jew, her reply was a matter-of-fact "Yes. Why not?"

For many survivors and their children, the Holocaust will continue to prove a barrier to healing the chasm of anger, mistrust, and fear between Jew and Gentile. For the first and second generation of the Holocaust, any attempt to distort the uniqueness of Jewish persecution during that period by shifting focus to the universal—Catholics, gypsies, homosexuals, soldiers of both the allies and the German army—and thereby implying that we were all victims is an affront, a denial of their suffering.

Many survivors are uncomfortable with the recent attention paid mostly by Jewish organizations to the recognition of Righteous Gentiles, those few non-Jews who risked their lives while assisting Jews. For survivors, this emphasis invokes an unwarranted symmetry (there were some bad Gentiles and there were some good Gentiles) when, in fact, the overwhelming majority of non-Jews actively participated or passively complied in the Final Solution—in most cases, pleased that someone was undertaking the task. Christians killed Jews, survivors simply assert.

Gentiles, as Anne Roiphe has pointed out, objectively view the Holocaust as another in a long chain of *human* horrors. For the Jew, the Holocaust is *personal* and unique, the culmination of Gentile hatred for the Jew.[10] This fundamentally different perspective will perpetuate the psychological distance and animosity between Jew and non-Jew. The divide will be further widened by the guilt and subsequent angry response of the Gentile as the Jew insists on pointing the finger at him.

Many children of survivors in my study experienced a developmental evolution of their feelings about being Jewish. For me, my perceptions of Gentiles have also evolved—from enemy, to stranger, to different. For Gentiles, particularly those in North America, Jews are not an issue. For children of survivors, Gentiles are.

7

In Case It Should
Happen Again

"My name is Joseph. It's an international name given to me
so if I have to flee it is easily translatable. Growing up, I was
repeatedly told to be a doctor so that if I have to escape a
place I can use those skills anywhere. My life has been a
preparation for the potential need to uproot myself at a
moment's notice. . . . Every day I heard about the Holocaust
and I've been getting ready for it to happen again."

It is not surprising that survivors' attitudes of mistrust and cynicism
and their fear of renewed persecution would be reflected in their
children. Still, I was astounded to find that almost three-quarters of
my participants, a generation once removed from the Holocaust, responded affirmatively to the question "Do you believe there could be
another attempted Jewish Holocaust?" When I asked other groups
who were not as intimately connected to the Holocaust the same
question, I usually received positive answers from only about 10 to 40
percent, with Jewish audiences at the upper end and non-Jewish
audiences at the lower end of this range.

The often-heard reassurances, such as "It could never happen
again," "It could never happen because we now have the State of
Israel, a refuge and a military power," "Jews are much more alert
now," "The world has geopolitically and technologically changed so
much," have not assuaged the anxiety of children of Holocaust survivors. Most participants in my study perceived the world to have
malicious intentions toward them as Jews. They felt isolated and in
danger.

When we witness a disaster such as an airplane crash, a fatal automobile accident, we may have the fleeting thought "There, but for the grace of God. . . ." In the service of self-preservation and to prevent paralysis, most of us quickly move away from our feelings of vulnerability. The continuous exposure to survivor parents, however, provokes an insecurity from which it is difficult to escape. A deep-seated identification with one's parents promotes the uneasy thought "It could have been me."

When they considered the possibility of another attempted Jewish Holocaust, the children of survivors I interviewed assumed a historical perspective. It may not occur tomorrow, next year, or in the immediate decades to come. But when one acknowledges the Jewish people's relationship to the non-Jewish world for the past two thousand years, one's understanding of periodic, violent, anti-Semitic outbreaks produces a certain outlook and expectation. And, as the world moves further away in time from the last destruction, its memory recedes and distorts, thereby adding greater probability to recurrence.

"When times are bad, the Jews have always been a scapegoat. If people don't keep the memory of the Holocaust alive, there could be another one. I may also think this because I've heard it from my parents. If you look at an Arafat, a Kaddafi, it's hard to believe that it couldn't happen again."

"I don't think in terms of we'll all be in concentration camps again. I get frightened when I hear of acts of anti-Semitic vandalism or neo-Nazi rallies. I can't believe the people of today would go to the lengths of concentration camps and isolation of the Jews, but emotionally I have an underlying fear that it could happen. I feel like I need the security blanket of Israel to go to so I guess that means I believe it might happen. Even though I know there aren't many neo-Nazis, I give them great significance in terms of the number of people they could potentially attract."

"I believe it could happen because I'm an educated person. History repeats itself. There are a lot of hate groups in the world and a lot of very educated, influential people in this world who don't like Jews. . . . I don't like Jews doing bad things that can be publicized. It scares me. It just gives them another reason. I want to believe that it's over and will never happen again but I'm still frightened."

"The Holocaust was a culmination of centuries of anti-Semitism. Jews have always been a scapegoat and they could be again. Anti-Semitism is still rampant. The United Nations devotes more energy to condemning Israel than any other issue. Moslems hate us. Christians hate us. Those factors which existed in the 1930s could exist again. People are capable of it. Hitler was a person. German Jews were very assimilated as American Jews are today. I'm sure they could not believe it could happen there. . . . We are just lucky right now."

Joseph, deeply affected by his Holocaust background, had obviously thought about this question before he had ever met me. His list of enemies was clear and seemingly rehearsed:

I don't think people are any different. Germans aren't particularly unique. Wherever Jews are (except Israel) they are a minority, they are vulnerable. Economically they have done well and, therefore, wherever someone might need a scapegoat, they would be ready-made. The Arabs would. Africa was ready to sever ties with Israel. South America is filled with Nazis. There are skinheads in the United States. The Japanese have anti-Israel propaganda and believe Jews to be a dangerous people. The United Nations said Zionists are racists. China has no relationship with Israel. Our friends are very few. . . . You only need a few bad people and the rest will follow. They just won't have any interest in opposing it. During World War II all those refugees who couldn't get out of Europe because no one would take them—the United States, Britain. Britain, such a civilized society. I recently read a book about goodness. I wanted to reassure myself that there are good people in the world.

Some of my respondents narrowly focused their gaze on the persecution of the Jews. They rigidly defined "us" and "them" and saw little commonality of human experience in these two distinct and, seemingly, eternally antagonistic groups. Other children of survivors extended their family's and people's history of victimization to engender a greater sensitivity to those who experience injustice, wherever they may be found. The general cynicism of this latter group of children fueled their predictions of future Holocausts to any potential scapegoat. People were cruel and easily influenced, they believed.

"I believe the world has learned much, but there are enough people who haven't and who could manage any type of Holocaust—Jewish, Black, East Indian. How can there be people who teach and write that the Holocaust never occurred and no one does anything about that? I have no faith in human kindness as a whole. Certainly, there could be another Jewish Holocaust. Or an Armenian one. Or a Japanese one. Or a nuclear one. I believe that history has made it obvious that hatred and persecution are a part of the human experience and that it would be naive to think otherwise. Israel has provided Jews with a new 'muscle' at this time, yet this muscle is not beyond damage or destruction."

"Although I would like to think that much of what occurred is unique to the cultural and historical milieu in Europe, I also believe that much of what happened relates to basic human traits. Large groups easily become infused with hate and turn into mindless mobs."

For the second generation, Israel provides a lightening rod for their fears and catastrophic expectations. Seemingly besieged from so many quarters, surrounded by enemies, with few, if any, true friends in sight, Israel represents, in many ways, the vulnerable Jew during the Holocaust. That they perceive Israel's position as precarious intensifies the insecurities of some children of survivors, despite their being thousands of miles from the Middle East. If the stronghold of the Jewish people, Israel, were to fall, could any Jew's safety, anywhere, be assured? When Israel is isolated from the international community, either politically or militarily, the fears of Jews around the world of another Holocaust are reflexively generated. When Israel appears strong, impermeable, and able to extend its protective wing even far outside of its borders (Entebbe, for example) Jews relax, somewhat.

Some children of survivors feel as though *they* have been through the Holocaust. In her doctoral dissertation, Fran Klein-Parker stated, "In many instances the adult children reported that they were acting like survivors themselves. One woman related, 'I walk around with a lot of impending doom. I lived with it growing up.' This need to deprive themselves as adults was also a replay of parental expectations of doom. . . . Many recalled that as children they were fearful of parents being captured again and of Hitler trying to destroy them also."[1]

Klein-Parker attributed the survivor-like actions and feelings of these children of survivors to an overidentification with their parents' experiences. I believe, however, there may be more to the adoption of a survivor stance by the second generation than mere identification. Children of survivors may feel guilt at having been excluded from the Holocaust that consumed their relatives.

In August 1987, my mother asked my sister and me to accompany her on a journey back to Poland, back to before. We spent one afternoon at Treblinka. After walking throughout the grounds, my mother and sister returned to the awaiting taxi. I lingered at the railroad siding where Jews disembarked at the pathway that would lead them to death. I thought of those days and nights. Bedlam. I wept. And then I experienced what was, for me, the most revelatory and jarring moment of my trip. As I started to leave, I felt a sudden tugging at me to remain. I felt an *obligation* to remain, to share the same fate as my brothers and sisters.

Why should I not have been involved? Why should I have been fortunate enough to have avoided the clutches of my family's tormentors? The following account by a child of survivors indicates a need to have been victimized during the Holocaust, and a desire to escape annihilation and prove oneself worthy of survival.

> My parents were affected by the war and I was affected by it. The war has affected me deeply, worse than my parents. A lot of times I felt that I had gone through the war myself. . . . The feeling is, my parents survived, am I as good as they are? For different reasons I thought I had to go fight in the war and very often I imagined myself being captured in Vietnam as a prisoner and escaping like my father did or surviving Vietnam. It's the thought of being captured and trying to escape to prove myself.[2]

Survivor guilt experienced by the second generation may induce fantasies and dreams of Nazi persecution. These images do not occur merely as a result of fears communicated by parent to child, nor are they simply a manifestation of an identification with the survivor parent. Rather, they may indicate a desire to participate in the victimization. The ongoing angst these children carry with them also reflects their *need* to suffer, to *not* be excluded from the Holocaust. Here, we may also more completely understand the extraordinarily high proportion of children of survivors who expect another Jewish Holocaust to occur. If one cannot be a part of the real event, one can assume the role of potential victim who is vigilant to the ongoing threat of another Holocaust. One can still perceive oneself to be in danger, even if that danger is not imminent.

A minority of my participants, a little more than one-fifth, did not believe that a Jewish Holocaust would occur again. (Less than a tenth provided an ambiguous response, neither affirming nor dismissing the possibility.) Yet, even for these children of survivors, emotional and intellectual responses to the question were often incongruent. While denying an overt threat, an underlying uneasiness inevitably emerged. "Everything is so transitory. Nothing is certain. Your life can be great one minute. In the next minute, it could all turn to ashes," remarked Joseph. While their view of life was not quite as bleak as Joseph's, the pessimism of other children of survivors emerged.

> "I don't *want* to believe it, and I don't really believe it will happen either. The superpowers have too much power and there is the rising status of various formerly persecuted minorities who remember what it was like being down so low. I do think though that the world's people *will* be destroyed in a major war and/or nuclear holocaust."

> "I don't think another Holocaust like that would be possible. I believe that the undercurrents of anti-Semitism that led to it are still present in the world today. There are groups of people here and in Europe who feel as much contempt for Jews as the Nazis did then. But there is such a heightened awareness of how inhuman and horrible the Holocaust was for Jews, there has been so much education and enlightenment about it and its causes, that it seems unlikely that it could happen again. Any government with such extremist policies that tried to exterminate Jews in great numbers would, I feel sure, be stopped by more reasonable powers in the world. And if not, then certainly by other Jews."

In 1979, Harvey Barocas and Carol Barocas wrote of children of survivors: "They seem to share an anguished collective memory of the Holocaust in both their dreams and fantasies reflective of recurrent references to their parents' traumatic experiences. These children wake up at night with terrifying nightmares of the Nazi persecution, with dreams of barbed wire, gas chambers, firing squads, torture, mutilation, escaping from enemy forces, and fears of extermination."[3] To the question "Do you ever have dreams which are Holocaust related?" slightly more than a third of my participants responded positively. A few subjects noted that they did not remember their dreams.

Several others reported dreams that could be viewed as originating from their unique background but which are very common among the general population as well, such as dreams of victimization. This latter group was not included in the number whose dreams clearly reflected themes originating in the Holocaust.

Approaches to dream interpretation have been diverse. For some theoreticians, dreams impersonate previous unconscious desires and/or conflicts. Other commentators have emphasized the forward-looking nature of dreams; that is, they may represent wishes for or fears of the future. Both of these orientations seem to illuminate the dynamics behind the dreams of children of Holocaust survivors.

For many in the second generation, certain Holocaust-related images periodically appear while they sleep. Dogs, trains, skeletons, Nazis, concentration camps, burnings, *appels* (the morning and evening lineup in concentration camps), relatives whom they never knew. They are searched for, chased, defiled, about to be murdered. They attempt to save others, and, with more or less success, extricate themselves from the jaws of death.

As an actor, perhaps Steve is unusually open to feelings and images that emerge from his unconscious:

> I have a fairly active dreamlife and I assume that much of it is somehow connected to the Holocaust, although usually not directly. There are a number of dreams that have been in the nature of escaping—running and being pursued. Because my father escaped from camps twice I feel that the connection lies there.
>
> As a child I often had a dream where I was on a fast-moving train and I was being pursued on this train. Chased from compartment to compartment. The other passengers sat in place and never took part in either pursuing me or stopping me or helping me. I ran through the train, bumped into people. All the time the train was racing, and I was frightened by the breakneck speed. Eventually I would be on top of the moving train, running, with my pursuers right behind me. Sometimes they would be in uniform and sometimes they wouldn't. There always came a point in the dream when I would be cornered or just about to be captured and would then kill one of my pursuers. I did this either by throwing him off the train or clubbing him to death with either an ax or some wooden club. These dreams happened often when I was a child, and they were always in two parts. The first part ended when I killed my pursuer, and then it was as if there was a break or blackout in the dream and I would be aware that the train was suddenly stopped—there was a

clearing—I was completely alone, the train was completely empty—no passengers, no pursuers—just me standing on the ground in the clearing. There was a wooded area off in the distance, and a small group of children would come out of the woods. There would be a little girl among them, and she would beckon for me to come to join them. I would be drawn to them but would be afraid to go along with them, and the dream would end with me being drawn but not quite being able to join the children.

This dream came often when I was younger—as a child and also as a young adult. I think the last time I had it I was in my mid-twenties. I remember that at least one time the little girl spoke. She said, "Allen, Allen, come here." And there was something hypnotic, alluring, sensual about the way she said the name "Allen." I always thought it was odd that she didn't know my name—or, rather, she did know my name—she completely recognized me, but the name was wrong and that made me very afraid and suspicious.

There have been other pursuit dreams, and in some of them I thought I was my father. Usually I would be running through woods, and sometimes there have been dogs chasing me as well. One time when I was tripping on LSD in Maine I hallucinated that I was my father and ran panicked through the woods as if I was him making his break from the camp.

Shortly after my mother died I believe I had a dream in which I became the sister, Dora, that my mother lost during her first six months at Buchenwald. Dora was seventeen and my mother was twelve. As they were being herded to the train my grandmother decided to break away from the line to try to get back to the house and find an infant brother who had been left behind. It was night, and before she made her break she said to Dora, "Take care of Luba (my mother), she's not very strong." Those were the last words my mother ever heard her mother say, and she always remembered and obsessed over them. She felt it was ironic that Dora weakened at Buchenwald and died quickly, while, she, the weak one, thrived and survived.

The night my mother died she kept calling out for her sister Dora. She had a terrible fever that kept climbing until it reached 107 and she went. In my dream, it is terribly hot. Both me and my mother are burning and I feel compelled to rescue her, but I know that the only way she can be saved is if no one else knows about it. My mother is deformed and grotesque and sweating and suffering terribly. Like in *Romeo and Juliet*, I fake her death. Everyone thinks she has died, but I know it's not true. I take her body to the ocean and somehow I get her onto a huge ice ship. It is like a huge houseboat but it is made completely out of ice and we both become cooled by the ice. I know, in this dream, that as long as we are on the boat made of ice we are safe, but that as soon as we leave the boat we will be burned and deformed. When we get on the boat my mother becomes transformed into a pretty young girl, the young girl she had been before, the young girl she was when I was a child. And I also become a pretty young girl, and we dance together on the boat made out of ice. Somehow, when having that dream, I am convinced that I am her sister Dora.

I was always fascinated by the grotesque photos from the camps, and sometimes in my dreams the people and animals take on the aspect of those skeletal survivors from the camps. I remember having a dream once where I'm riding a horse, running among a herd of horses, and all of them become skeletons with dripping flesh falling from their bones and I'm on the one in the middle, horrified and desperate to get away but unable to dismount because of all the other horses and dripping flesh surrounding me.

The above descriptions by a forty-one-year-old man echo many of the thematic elements found in the dreams of children of survivors. Fear and suspicion abound. While the subject was running from antagonists, passengers stood idly by offering no assistance. He felt isolated from others. He may also have been ambivalent (because of both survivor guilt and a desire for safety) about joining the other children caught in the vortex of the Holocaust. The girl beckoned to him, but perhaps it was not really his turn, he believed. Dogs, skeletons, burnings, dripping flesh intruded. There were attempts to undo the mother's disrupted childhood and restore her to a prewar state, as well as a desire to reverse the death of a relative (Dora) and return her to the parent. This particular participant fought back and was able to escape his enemies. Other children of survivors often display a powerlessness, ineffectualness, and an expectation of the inevitability of death in their dreams. Sheilah, a thirty-eight-year-old child of survivors, reported: "In most of those Holocaust dreams I am in life-threatening situations and [sometimes] those I love are as well. Someone is after me and wants to harm me and I feel helpless. I want to scream but nothing happens."

The following accounts are representative of dreams narrated by children of Holocaust survivors. Again, common themes emerged from the unconscious of these individuals: a fear of Nazi-like persecution; placing oneself in perilous situations that were analogous to those their parents endured; a desire to undo parental trauma; and a need to be sheltered from harm in contrast to their parents, who had not been protected.

Many children of survivors reported experiencing Holocaust-related nightmares with greater frequency when they were younger. There may be several explanations for this phenomenon. In general, we feel more vulnerable during childhood. As we age, we have the opportunity and tools needed to acquire greater mastery over our anxieties. In addition, many survivors have only relatively recently provided more details of their Holocaust life to their offspring. This supplemental information and input of reality may have contributed to diminishing the solicitude of the second generation. The following dreams were all reported by women.

"I have had bad dreams involving concentration camp scenes only rarely in life. I think I had a few nightmares like that as a child, but I really don't remember the content or the details. Recently, after seeing *Shoah* for the first time, I had terrible nightmares for several nights. The part of the dream that seemed to keep recurring was terrifying. I was in the back of a huge truck, the kind that was used to kill Jews by leading an exhaust hose into the back of the truck and choking the Jews with the carbon-monoxide fumes. In my dreams, I was either with my husband and son or sometimes only with my son. The scenario was just horrible: people screaming, moaning, fainting, defecating from fear, trying in vain to open the back of the truck and get out. . . . I had never before heard of this particular means of killing the Jews, and it apparently made a real impression on me in the film when people were describing it."

"I had more Holocaust-related dreams when I was a child. I rarely have them now. The dreams were usually ones where I was being pursued. There was always that need to find a place to hide. I never fought back. I was always running or hiding. I remember a dream from when I was in college. I went to see the play *Bent*. My father had also lifted stones from one place to another in a concentration camp. I dreamt I was in one of these camps. There were a lot of people I knew. I woke up when I was about to be killed. After the dream I realized I couldn't marry my non-Jewish boyfriend, that he would never be able to understand my dream."

"When I was five to ten years old, I had a recurring dream. I was on a bus and I would see my murdered grandfather on the street, and my neighborhood would become an eastern European street. I ran after him and brought him home to my mother."

"I had a recurrent dream as a child. My parents owned a candy store and they were always talking about hoodlums coming into the store to steal. I thought hoodlums were like Nazis. These bodies that looked like hoods would come into my house and disrupt everything. . . . I played with dolls when I was a child, those dolls which fit into one another. When I played I fantasized the dolls hiding inside their mother from the Nazis. These dolls are the only thing I still have from my childhood."

"In my dreams I see myself standing in line in winter, barely clothed, waiting to be counted in a concentration camp. I had these dreams frequently in my twenties but less so now."

The following dream of Paula, a nineteen-year-old child of survivors, was a clear manifestation of ongoing fears fed by her family's Holocaust background. (This individual also responded vehemently in the affirmative to the question "Do you believe there could be another attempted Jewish Holocaust?") The protagonist, unable to escape, and unable to be protected by her parents, is murdered.

I once dreamt that I was in my house and my family was there with me. There was a knock on the door and my father went out to get it. Meanwhile, my mother took two babies wrapped up in white blankets in her arms and ran into the bathroom in my parents' bedroom. (I assume the babies were my sister and I.) They shot my father in the living room and searched the rest of the house for our family. They searched the den, my bedroom that my sister and I shared, my hallway, and found nothing. I was scared that they would find us, even though they started to leave my house. I quickly jumped out of the bathroom and peeked out the bedroom door. They all had their backs toward me. I tried to run into the den because I knew they had already checked there. I thought I'd be safe when all of a sudden one spotted me and yelled, "There she is!" As I reached the doorway to my den, I was shot. I woke up choking and unable to breathe. I've had other nightmares, but none that I could remember so clearly.

Four prevalent themes (feelings of vulnerability associated with one's Jewish identity, the inevitability of the destruction of the Jewish people, the feared inability of one's parents to provide a safeguard, survivor guilt and the desire to participate in the Holocaust) illustrative of children of survivors were reflected in the dream of Janice, a thirty-year-old participant. One might also interpret the denouement as an indication of the child's desire to offer herself in place of her parents, thereby sparing them the torment which they had undergone.

In particular I remember one dream which I had at about age twenty-one as a university student. I was a child of eleven or twelve in my dream. My two brothers, parents, my grandmother, and I were all at a large gathering of people inside a large auditorium. Hitler was there in uniform and he was moving amongst the various cliques of talking crowds and smiling, greeting, shaking hands. My family knew what our fate could potentially be, so we had to conceal the fact that we were Jewish. I kept worrying how I would be able to smile superficially at this horrible man and conceal my hatred and fear of him. My father urged me to be strong. There were huge red-and-white Nazi banners with black swastikas hung throughout the auditorium. Hitler was handing out bars of chocolate when he met families with children. Hitler moved toward my family to greet us. I was also nervous because I had a Star of David around my neck which I kept trying to hide inside my shirt, but it kept showing itself. Hitler shook hands with my parents, and I felt ill with panic. He moved toward my brother and me and ruffled our hair, telling my parents that we were such cute kids. Then he handed us candy bars.

At the next scene of the dream my family and I were walking down a long, *long*, carpeted hallway toward an exit to the building. After we exited, we would be able to breathe a sigh of relief and go home. As I walked with my family I somehow turned to look in back of us. Walking in a group behind us was a hologram—in black and white—of Jewish prisoners silently marching toward the camp. They all had Jewish stars tied around their arms. My family was oblivious to them and, in any case, there was no speaking in this part of the dream. The prisoners were walking in a group behind us and stepping together almost mechanically. The more I glanced back at them, sympathetically, the further I fell out of step with my family. Soon, I had lost pace with my family and I fell into step with the Jewish concentration camp prisoners. A mechanical door opened and my family, assuming I was with them, walked out to freedom. Before my group reached the exit, the mechanical gate shut loudly. I was trapped and was to receive the same fate as these prisoners.

One might view the perilous situations in which children of survivors placed themselves during their dreams as evidence of their survivor guilt, their need to suffer as well. Jerry, a twenty-two-year-old dental student, described his Holocaust-related dreams in the following manner: "I risk my well-being or suffer something. They are usually heroic dreams involving my coming through danger." This respondent's success in eluding harm served to assuage his underlying fears of vulnerability. His "heroic" stance also served to justify his survival while so many others perished.

Dreams represent a compromise. Defense mechanisms serve to distort underlying unconscious wishes so that they may be acceptable and accessible to us as we sleep. More conscious reverie allows additional access to buried psychic material. While I did not ask subjects about their daytime fantasies, other sources have indicated their occurrence and inclusion of themes that appeared in the previously described dreams.

Helen Epstein, a journalist and child of survivors, wrote:

> I became an American child. I watched Mickey Mouse Club, played baseball, and memorized the score of every musical on Broadway. My teachers were pleased with me. I had several "best" friends. I seemed to be as well adjusted as any other little girl growing up on the Upper West Side of New York. But when my mother took me to Carnegie Hall, I would often imagine a group of men in black coats bursting into the auditorium and shooting everybody dead. Other times I went to St. Patrick's cathedral, crossed myself and lit four candles for my grandparents. When I rode the subways I pretended the trains were going to Auschwitz.[4]

The belief of the second generation in the likelihood of another Holocaust affects their outlook on life, their deepest fears, their interpersonal relationships with Jews and non-Jews alike. It also engenders an unusually meaningful psychological and physical relationship between children of survivors and the State of Israel. A little more than three-quarters of my sample had visited Israel at least once. (This contrasts sharply with the fact that over 80 percent of American Jews have never been to Israel.) Slightly more than a quarter of my sample (excluding those participants who had been born in Israel) had either visited Israel more than five times or lived in Israel continuously for more than six months or both.

For many Jews, Israel is testimony to the endurance of their people. Those of my group who repeatedly returned to that country may indeed have experienced an inordinate need to reaffirm their people's survival, as well as their own existence. Those most emotionally involved with the Holocaust seem also to have been the ones who felt the most psychologically invested in and connected to the State of Israel.

Within the Jewish community, Holocaust survivors are, perhaps, the staunchest supporters of Israel. They travel there, are generous in their financial aid, and view geopolitical decisions of their host country through a partisan lens—simply, Is it good or bad for Israel? The pride of survivors has been resuscitated by the Jewish homeland. The State of Israel's existence exclaims their own presence.

Understandably, most survivors experience an identification with Israel's ongoing struggle to overcome its enemies. As Israel is perceived as the bulwark averting another Holocaust, the outcome of that battle has very personal ramifications for the felt vulnerability of survivors in the Diaspora. And, for some survivors, the creation of a Jewish state may have provided some small compensation for their previous losses. Moreover, it allowed a partial psychological undoing of the Holocaust while ironically posing a reminder of the Shoah and the fragility of the Jewish people as a result of its continuous precarious position.

The second generation have imbibed their parents' feelings for Israel. Stimuli associated with Israel—Israeli music, the national anthem of Israel—provoke a rush of emotional responses. Secular, westernized, sophisticated, educated children of survivors cry when they first spy the coastline of Israel from thirty thousand feet in the air, kiss the ground at Lod Airport as they disembark from their craft. Disagreements over policy or reactions to abrasive Israelis do not diminish their commitment to the security of the State of Israel. The reflections of children of survivors presented here were obtained during the uprising on the West Bank and Gaza in 1988 and 1989, a period of intense negative publicity and controversy even within the Jewish community regarding governmental conduct.

For children of survivors, Israel provides security for Jews everywhere. It is the buffer between them and their enemies, wherever they may be. Because of the historically tenuous position of Jews in the Diaspora, Israel is viewed as the only, reliable, safe haven for Jewish people.

> "Israel is very important to me. I've grappled with whether or not to live there. I think Israel is central to the survival of the Jewish people. I could understand it if my children wanted to live there even though I would be far from them. If Israel were to go, I would feel extremely vulnerable. It would be terrifying for me. And I see the possibility of its destruction at any time. The world is filled with Israel's enemies. Israel's enemies are my enemies."

"I don't like Israelis. I find them very arrogant. . . . I associate Israel with Hebrew School and I hated Hebrew School. . . . I am, however, deeply concerned about Israel and the status of Jewish security."

"I have never been to Israel. I feel like Israel is a relative that I have to visit. I feel strongly about Israel's need to exist. *I* need Israel to exist as a place of refuge in case anything awful ever happened again. I don't have a need to go there, but it's a comfort to know it's there. I worry more than other Jews I know when things are tough there."

Israel also provides a veritable link to past generations of Jews. Because of their enhanced sensitivity to cultural continuity, children of survivors, therefore, feel an especially keen attachment. For Sheilah, the mother of two quoted earlier, Israel was family. "I have been to Israel four times and I have a very strong emotional connection to it. When the plane lands, I am always moved to tears. It's very much a place of who I am. Walking into Yad Vashem makes me feel at home. I am with people who identify with what I have been through and who are like me. I have never felt as comfortable or as at home as when I am there. Just as the Holocaust is so much a part of who I am, so is Israel."

"I spent some time, a year, in Israel the year after I graduated from high school back in 1976," Clara, the high school teacher mentioned earlier, recounted. Her feelings before leaving, she recalled, were mixed. In part she felt that she was showing contrived enthusiasm for a land she had never been to. Her curiosity was aroused; yet Israel remained an idea, an intangible as yet unexperienced and therefore impossible to love.

I metamorphosized as I got off the plane at Lod and was greeted by a rush of quick-speaking Israeli brusqueness. Yes, these people were like all the rude, pushy, idiosyncratic and yet somehow lovable and honest Israeli Hebrew School teachers I'd been plagued with for so many years. Israel seemed distinctive and peculiar to anything I'd ever experienced. . . . The people were characters but *real* people. And when I went for a walk with an American friend one day in an endless, open field away from our kibbutz, the sky was so blue and cloudless, it seemed so close to the ground. It occurred to me that it was so fitting because this is Israel. The heaven touched the earth. We rolled on the ground and cried, clenching the rich soil in our hands without speaking.

The second cathartic experience came on my first visit to the Wailing Wall. I was overcome with emotion and at that moment felt the full beauty of all Judaism and my intrinsic link between the line of Jews which came before me and all those who will come thereafter.

Some relatives of survivors emigrated from eastern Europe to Palestine before the Shoah. In addition, after World War II, approximately one half of displaced Jews made their way to the Middle East to begin life anew in a Jewish homeland. As a result, many of the children of survivors I interviewed had some relatives in Israel, a circumstance that added to their psychological closeness to the country and, indirectly, promoted a sense of having a personal, physical presence there as well.

> "I have been to Israel three times. In addition, my mother's whole family lives there. So all my life I have heard a lot about my many aunts and uncles and cousins in Israel. I met them, and the names took on faces and personalities. . . . There is also the feeling of Israel being a homeland. This is comforting to me. I feel proud of all the Jews have done to build up a desert country and make it as successful as they have."

> "I have never been to Israel but I have many distant relatives who live there, and my family is very close to some of them. I have one cousin, Dov, who was born in Israel and who lived with us here in the United States when I was twelve to fourteen years old. Dov was my age and we were very close, but after those two years, his family moved back to Israel. In the 1973 war Dov was killed and through him I have a personal attachment to the State of Israel. . . . My feelings are not tremendously close or personal, but because of the Holocaust and because of my cousin I do feel an affinity with Israel and a vested interest in its survival. . . . I am very critical of many of its policies, particularly regarding the Palestinian situation. My politics, in general, are left wing and, if it weren't for the Holocaust, I would probably be more critical of Israel than I am."

> "I was twenty when I made my first trip to Israel. I remember seeing all the soldiers with guns on the buses and in the streets and thinking, 'These are the Macabees, fighting for my Jewish land, fighting for me.' I felt a rush, a strength. . . . I feel guilty that I have not fought in Israel's wars to defend the Jewish people. And by engaging present enemies I guess I would have felt I was engaging past ones as well. . . . In Israel I always feel like I am

really among my people. Israel is my home. For me, living in America is like living as a displaced person."

As their past involuntarily intrudes with unsettling frequency on their present, survivors attempt to live lives that are as normal as possible. Children of survivors also live in an outwardly commonplace fashion. Direct and indirect evidence indicates, however, that many in the second generation function with some anticipatory anxiety regarding the future. "They" are committed to our destruction. It is only a matter of time before another strike occurs. These fears do not incapacitate, but they do produce an uneasiness that is readily stimulated by any confirmation of the world's antipathy to the Jew.

Can I Believe in God?

For those who in this long exile are critical of God, believing that He has forsaken them. May they experience God's providential care, His mercy and grace.

—Rabbenu Yona

We received the Torah on Sinai
and in Lublin we gave it back.
Dead men don't praise God,
the Torah was given to the living.
And just as we all stood together
at the giving of the Torah,
so did we all die together in Lublin.

—Jacob Glatstein, "Dead Men Don't Praise God"

Faith. Perhaps its most striking quality has been durability. For millennia, man has believed in God or gods. This expression is testimony to a variety of psychological needs. It serves as an organizing principle, an explanation for the simple, the complex, the contradictory. It salves our insecurities, above all, our feelings of powerlessness and subsequent fear. If only some otherworldly, stronger than human force would watch over us. It has also provided justification for the unleashing of our own aggressive impulses against our fellow man, as we assume that our group is right and better, while the other, foreign, group is misguided and inferior.

The idea of God is not a comfort to me, but a taunt.

According to the Bible, the Jews are the Chosen People. God's covenant with them is a unique, special one. In my calmest moments, historical facts would seem to contradict this notion. In my outrage, I find the idea to be a cruel hoax. (Will my enemy order me to drop my pants, find the symbol of my covenant with God, and, then, after viewing the evidence of my crime, shoot me?) Rumor has it that the Jews were not God's first choice, that He offered the Torah to others before us but was turned down. After much deliberation and skepticism, Moses and his crowd accepted it. Would they have, had they foreseen the resulting tragedies that would befall them?

In the face of the most pernicious persecution, we persisted in our attempts to obey God's laws, asking rabbis for their rulings and interpretations of the Divine Will. In reviewing questions of Jewish law that arose in the midst of the Holocaust, Irving Rosenbaum recounts the following episode:

> During the Holocaust period, a group of Jews were hiding in a bunker from the Nazis who were conducting a "search and destroy" operation. It was certain that they would all be killed if the Germans discovered their hiding place. Suddenly an infant, who was among those concealed in the bunker, began to cry. It was impossible to quiet him. If the Nazis heard his cries, they would be discovered and all would be lost. While they were wondering whether it would be all right to stifle the cries with a pillow, since the child might suffocate, one of the men in the bunker seized one and covered the child's face. After the Germans had left and they were safe, they removed the pillow and found, to their dismay, that the infant had suffocated.[1]

Tenaciously preoccupied with man's obligations under the law of God, Jews approached Rabbi Efrati and asked if this man's action was permissible, since it was done to save the life of others.

Jews, fearing God's disapproval, attempting to find moral order, assuage their conscience, still the trembling of their soul, look for an answer from a theological master. Why should man, why should Jews, be forced to wrestle with such questions?

People of the Book, People of the Law.

I anticipate the Jewish holidays, particularly the Days of Awe, Rosh Hashanah, and Yom Kippur, and I feel a subliminal apprehension. I am drawn to the synagogue. I begin to read, to pray, responding habitually to the stimuli of the surroundings. I attempt intercourse with past generations who echoed the same words, for my identification as a Jew is primarily a historical one, a communion with a people.

In order to feel closer to my people, I use my imagination. It has been approximately fifty generations since Aaron, Moses' brother, the man from whom I derive. I picture fifty individuals lined up, with him at one end and me at the other, and then I feel close. Fifty seems like a small number, a short line.

I think of the swaying Jews around the world who are intoning the same prayers, at the same time. I feel a part of this huddled mass clinging to one another for safety, for identity, for hope.

But soon I am stopped short by the words staring at me from the prayer book. And every page I turn seems to flout, to mock me.

God is gracious and merciful.

God is righteous.

God is kind and compassionate.

God has chosen us from all the peoples. He loved us and found favor in us.

God protects all who love Him.

The words become stuck in my throat. They kindle my anger. I cannot read on.

There are those who would deny anyone who did not suffer through the Holocaust the right to doubt, to challenge, "Where was God?" Only a survivor's response is an authentic one, they assert. Furthermore, they would implore, how could one reject the existence of God when many survivors, despite their suffering, retained their unwavering devotion? To deny God's existence would imply a desecration of the faithful who intoned the sacred Shema, "Hear O Israel, the Lord is God, the Lord is One," as the gas fumes spread throughout the locked chambers.

Calamitous events often provoke doubt about the presence or nature of God by the believers who suffered and those who observed their suffering. Survivors have succumbed to this uncertainty. Yet, survivors who have been left with a troubling skepticism or even those whose faith was completely exhausted, nevertheless, strongly urged their children to continue Jewish tradition.[2] (This ambivalent communication may partially explain the fact that more than three-quarters of my sample reported having attended synagogue last Yom Kippur, while less than a tenth are religiously observant. There is an adherence to custom among the second generation, but a vacuum of fundamental belief in religious precepts.) Survivors' loss of religious conviction, despite the enhanced Jewish identity forced upon them, may prove a severe diluent for their children and the generations that will follow, "for while the Jews are a nation, a history, a culture, a tradition, a people, a memory, their religion, the one they held onto through inquisition after inquisition, the one that they passed on to their children knowing that it marked them for danger and limitation, is the glue, the sinew the connecting tissue binding Jew to Jew, Jew to history."[3]

Many survivors seem to have found it difficult to disavow God completely or discontinue their customary behavior. Having experienced so many losses, they refuse to disengage from this anchor, this source of support, this connection to their parents and grandparents. And, for them, perhaps God still maintains a buffer against unbridled Evil—for some did survive. Finally, they may believe that if He allowed them to survive, perhaps they *deserved* to live. At the very least, most survivors struggle with God, and, in the process, express their anger.

"I go to synagogue to accuse God. I used to go to ask forgiveness of my sins. Now I demand He ask forgiveness for His."

"I go to synagogue to remind Him I owe Him nothing. He owes me."[4]

The second generation also wrestles with God. As their confidence in His ability or willingness to protect His children is shaken, their vulnerability is felt more acutely. And, if he *could* have intervened but chose not to, why the lack of response? If He saved one or two miraculously, why didn't He save more? The most disturbing question, of course, would involve God's complicity in the Holocaust. Why did He do this to us?

> "As a child I always had a strong belief in God. My parents were in such a terrible situation and they were rescued by God. The fact that they seemed to have such a strong belief after the Holocaust meant that I should assume there is a God as well. . . . But now it doesn't make sense to me. If there is a God and if the Jews are the Chosen People, how could He do this to us? I don't believe that if I am a good Jew and a good person that God will protect me. The Holocaust has caused me to be more skeptical."

> "It's a paradox. How could a merciful God who considers us His Chosen People let this happen to us? At the same time, there are those who survived and survived at His mercy. I personally have faith in God."

> "My father is a cantor, was brought up as an Orthodox Jew. Once, before he underwent a major surgery, he admitted to me that he had asked himself, 'If there was a God, why was he in the camps?' I guess since then I have asked the same question."

Human beings need to believe there is someone who will protect them from the vicissitudes of life, the evil in man, perhaps even their own self-destructive impulses. As young children, we look to our parents as our guardians. As we age, we transfer some of that responsibility to God. Perhaps because of their enhanced sense of vulnerability arising from their Holocaust background, many children of survivors *want* to believe in God.

> "My belief in God comes from years of Sunday school and religious training outside the home more than from inside the home. I wonder if there could be a God if the Holocaust happened. I'm more superstitiously than religiously Jewish. I believe that if I don't believe in God, something bad might happen to me."

> "I know that despite all the horror in the world I choose to believe there is a God. He is the one Truth, the one Goodness. If I continue to believe this, I can rationalize bad things happening. I can be resilient and continue to have hope. Without hope, life isn't worth living. Somehow, to me, God represents a basic goodness and hope."

> "I believe in God very strongly. I *need* to believe in God because of the Holocaust. I need to believe there is someone to ask help of."

> "I grew up in a very secular home. As a child, it disturbed me that my father never went to synagogue. He would say to me, 'There is no God. There was a Holocaust.' People need to believe in God. It helps them, makes them better people. It gives me a good feeling to pray in synagogue, not because I think God will help me, but it gives me a good feeling."

Sitting at the table, on Passover night, at the home of an Orthodox rabbi, I asked him how he explained the Holocaust to himself. "I do not know," he answered. "We cannot understand all of God's ways. We are mere mortals. However, some have suggested it occurred because Jews at that time were not sufficiently observant. They had strayed from adherence to the Law, and were punished as a result." I am appalled by his notion of God. Didn't Christians use a similar argument to sustain and condone their anti-Semitism through the ages? And, would not an invocation of God's punishment seem to absolve Christians of responsibility for their crimes? Yet, the Prophetic tradition of blaming Jews for the catastrophes which befall them endures. The assimilationist tendencies of the Jews of Germany and eastern Europe are said to have provoked the wrath of God.[5] And, the Chofetz Chaim adds, when Torah is lost, the evil inclination manifests itself. Rabbi Joseph Duber Soloveitchik (1820–1892) counsels that the distance between Israel and other nations must be observed. When Jews get too close, God has the Gentiles push them back.[6]

Fortunately, there is also Eliezer Berkovits's *Faith after the Holocaust.* "The idea that the Jewish martyrology through the ages can be explained as divine judgment is obscene. Nor do we for a single moment entertain the thought that what happened to European Jewry in our generation was divine punishment for sins committed by them. It was injustice absolute; injustice countenanced by God."[7]

For many, however, the question is not Where was God? but Where was man? The indifference of the international community to Jewish refugees, both before and during World War II, has been thoroughly documented. The hostility toward Jews in many Western quarters, including the United States and England, manifested itself in strict immigration quotas. Public pronouncements of antipathy toward Jews and justifications for the violence unleashed upon them abounded. The Jews must have done something wrong. This was simply retribution.

Perhaps the most rational, humane argument for the coexistence of God and the Holocaust rests on the acknowledgment of man's freedom of choice. The assertion of man's free will does not necessarily imply a less powerful Divinity. Rather, some theologians insist that human beings can exist only because God renounces the use of his prerogative over them. Indeed, there are times when God is inexplicably absent from history and chooses to turn His face away, "conceal His Countenance (*Hester Panim*)."[8]

Eliezer Berkovits stated:

This is the inescapable paradox of divine providence. While God tolerates the sinner, he must abandon the victim; while he shows forbearance with the wicked, he must turn a deaf ear to the anguished cries of the violated. This is the ultimate tragedy of existence: God's very mercy and forbearance, his very love for man, necessitates the abandonment of some men to a fate that they may well experience as divine indifference to justice and human suffering. It is the tragic paradox of faith that God's direct concern for the wrongdoer should be directly responsible for so much pain and sorrow on earth. . . .

If man is to be, God himself must respect his freedom of decision. If man is to act on his own responsibility, without being continually over-awed by divine supremacy, God must absent himself from history.[9]

It is not only the nature of God but, indeed, the nature of human-kind that is crucial to our understanding of this central formulation. For, to take the dialectic one step further, there could be no righteous men if within them there were no potential for malice. It is toward man, and not God, that the accusation is directed by many children of survivors.

> "I believe that God places us on earth but does not *determine* our actions. He simply judges us by how we live."

> "I don't believe in any *intervening* God. Still, God is an important metaphor in my daily life. I live with the motto that one should act *as if* a God exists. The Holocaust is simply one small reason for nonbelief in the traditional, creating, intervening God."

> "The Holocaust has not affected my belief in God. I believe there is a higher power than us and that the Holocaust was a human manifestation of evil and not God's punishment or God's will."

A quarter of the participants in this study reported that they did not believe in God. For some, a lack of faith was characterized as unrelated to the Holocaust. For others, the silence from above during those horrific events fueled their disbelief. For a few, the question of God sparked the ventilation of anger during our interview.

> "I don't believe there was a God before the Holocaust and I certainly don't believe that there is one now. I might be wrong, but even if I am and God exists, I'm sure that he or she doesn't have anything to do with the workings of the natural world."

"It's not simply the Holocaust. It's our entire history that leads me not to believe in God. I was brought up very Orthodox, but I had too much doubt and asked too many questions in school."

"If there is one, he—or she—has quite a laissez-faire attitude."

"I'm a disbeliever. I'm a skeptic and a cynic because of the Holocaust. If there is a God and he let it happen, he's got to be an awfully sick guy."

"I don't really believe in God. I would have to call myself an agnostic. I'd like to believe. It would be comforting somehow to believe in a divine being and in heaven, but I just can't buy the whole idea. I'm too skeptical, I suppose. . . . I think one of the reasons for my skepticism has to stem from the Holocaust. Since childhood, I've asked myself this: If there is a God and he's a good and loving God, how could he let such a horrible thing happen to the Jews? How could he let innocent people, even little children, suffer so much? I have never found an answer."

Only a handful of subjects found their faith completely intact, unshaken by the events of the Holocaust. Gary, a thirty-five-year-old stockbroker, voiced the following representative statements of this group: "I believe there is a God. I believe the Holocaust was an aberration. I believe God loves the Jews and wants the Jews to survive. The Holocaust has not led me to the conclusion that because there was a Holocaust, there is no God. Maybe someday we'll understand how this was able to happen given there is a God."

When all explanations falter, when reality seems to contradict otherworldly speculation, when the pious themselves shake their heads in exasperation and despair, there is a convenient, albeit uneasy, fallback position. Silence. And then the homilies:

As mere mortals we cannot possibly fully understand his design.

The Holocaust is merely one piece of a grand, ever-evolving mosaic.

Our knowledge is incomplete as we only know about this world and not of the world to come. Our fourscore years on this earth are but a moment in time compared to the infinity of the hereafter. Good men will be rewarded, evil men punished.

The notion of God invites concepts of good and evil forces in the world. It also creates categories of good people and bad people, those who obey His wishes and those who dismiss them. My maternal grandfather's family in Lublin strictly adhered to religious precepts. My uncle, his son, a survivor of the Majdanek death camp, had been schooled throughout his childhood and adolescence at various yeshivas. Contrary to Rabbi Harold Kushner's modern assertions (rationalizations?) in *When Bad Things Happen to Good People* that God does not control all worldly events and that there are no causal explanations for many outcomes—particularly, harmful ones to good people—my uncle grew up believing in an omnipotent and omnipresent deity.

In the postwar world of America, my uncle regularly attended a Conservative synagogue, imposed a Jewish education on his children, visited Israel, and donated to Jewish causes. I recently asked him about the effects of the Holocaust on his belief in God. To my surprise, he responded that he had lost all faith. Much of his anger was directed at his formerly revered yeshiva teachers and rabbis who had urged their students to put their trust and life in God's hands. The more fervent the student, therefore, the more passive was his response to persecution. At one point my uncle remarked: "The best did not survive. The scholars, the righteous, the religiously observant, the sensitive, the gentle, all went rather naively and meekly to their death. You had to have a bit of larceny in your soul in order to survive." I have since heard this theme echoed by many other survivors.

Survivors attempt to find meaning in their suffering and in the loss of so many loved ones. They imbue the murders with a holiness, a divine spirit. They refer to those extinguished as having died Kiddush HaShem, as a means of sanctifying God. The misnomer, however, is obvious. At other times, Jews were given a choice of conversion. Their refusal to bend their knee to another deity was, indeed, an affirmation of their one God. The persecutors of the Holocaust were uninterested in theological finepoints. Their aim was simply destruction. Jews were not given options.

The dilemma for me is apparent and urgent. How am I to reconcile my fierce desire to maintain, indeed, intensify my identity as a Jew, in spite of my skepticism, at best, and incredulity, at worst, about the existence of God? Ultimately, how do I move *beyond* a narrow definition of Jewishness predicated on being a member of a group that was purposefully persecuted and almost annihilated in an unprecedented manner?

I study Jewish history, ancient and modern. I inhale Jewish culture by my attention to Jewish symbols—mezuzahs on my doorposts, a yahrzeit candle at the anniversary of my father's death, Jewish art, books, and music in my home, taking opportunities to speak Yiddish with family members or friends. I celebrate the appointed holidays, consciously performing rituals as my ancestors had done for centuries.

And I spend time with Hasidim. Another paradox. For while I do not share their fervent religious beliefs, I find myself attracted. I spend time with the Lubavitchers, particularly during the holidays, Simchat Torah, Hanukkah, and Rosh Hashanah. I watch a four-hour Yiddish discourse by the Lubavitcher rebbe on cable television. I walk the streets of their neighborhoods in Jerusalem, entering their small shuls, watching them interact, initiating a conversation in Yiddish about almost anything while waiting at a bus stop simply to feel close.

They are my contact with pre-Holocaust Lublin and eastern Europe. They are my slaughtered family whom I never had an opportunity to know. They are a dam attempting to hold back the pressures of assimilation and the disappearance of an epoch of Jewish life that I sentimentalize.

When I was younger I would seize any conversation with a rabbi and use the occasion to spew forth the question, the challenge. Driving to a funeral with a prominent Brooklyn Orthodox rabbi, having Passover seder with the rabbi of the largest Orthodox synagogue in Los Angeles, sitting in the study of the head of a yeshiva in Jerusalem, I would ask, "How could God let it happen?"

I hoped that my question was a riddle, that I would receive an answer that would quiet my doubts, excise my anger, attenuate my sadness, at least provide some meaningful framework. I knew relatively little theology or Bible. Perhaps there was some passage, some commentary. Perhaps someone so steeped in belief and rabbinic history could synthesize a response. On the other hand, if my question did not provoke an adequate response, I would have more fuel for an atheistic position. In the end, their answer was always the same: "To believe in God is a matter of faith."

As I grew older, I ceased my interrogation of others and grappled with the question myself. Perhaps my rebelliousness and anger had diminished. I began to understand that *I* must find a satisfying answer and resolution to my despair.

I try now to be open to the answer. I have substituted one uncertainty for another, as I can no longer call myself an atheist. Perhaps there is a Supreme Mover. I look for myself.

But I wish I would receive some sign.

9

The Third Generation

"I will try to make the world a less scary place for my daughter. I would like to insure that she has enough strength to not feel like a victim."

I waited until I was thirty-five to get married and have a child. I regret that my father, who passed away when he was fifty-seven, did not live to see his granddaughter. His heart gave out. Too many survivors die young, their bodies prematurely exhausted.

Death and life.

Rachel was born at Cedars Sinai Medical Center, located in an affluent section of Los Angeles. The environment was antiseptic, the surrounding high-tech machinery poised to avert complications or death; the people assisting were eager to bring this Jewish child into the world. My wife, Rebecca, had the freedom to scream when in pain, crying tears of joy at the result of her labor. I was by her side throughout, encouraging and protecting. After she emerged, Rachel was immediately given Rebecca's life-affirming breast. Mother and child bonded for what promised to be a long life together.

I am reminded of other scenarios. Mengele ordering a new mother's breasts bound to prevent the feeding of her newborn. How long could an infant live without food? he wondered. A mother administering a fatal morphine injection to her baby in order to forestall her own selection to the gas chamber. And a story from Auschwitz:

It was already dark when we arrived at the block. The women took us to the woman in labor. Mancy told her to lie on the ground under the board bed. She herself hid there too. "Remember," she said to her quietly, "you are forbidden to utter a sound. Everything has to take place in complete silence. Nobody should know that you are giving birth." She told me to bring her a bucket of cold water. She put it next to her.

"Sit next to me. You will be my helper," she said to me.

Two women stood near the bed. One of them was guarding the entrance to the block.

The birth started. The woman bit her lips in pain until she drew blood. But she did not utter even one sound. She held my hands so tightly that afterwards I had black and blue marks. Finally, the baby was born. Mancy put her hand over his mouth so he would not cry, and then she put his head in the bucket of cold water. She was drowning him like a blind kitten. I felt faint. I had to get out from under the bed.

"The baby was born dead," Mancy said. Later, she wrapped the dead baby in an old shirt, and the woman who was guarding the entrance took the baby and left to put it on a pile of corpses. The mother was saved.[1]

It is a year after Rachel's birth, 7:30 in the morning. Rachel, indicating her night has ended, lets out a soft cry, summoning me. She is standing, shaking her crib. As I approach her that day my vision blurs. I see murdered babies, emaciated babies, babies with their head crushed after being battered against the wall. I am in Lublin, 1942. My legs wobble. My disorientation passes quickly as I focus once again and see Rachel, clad in her Daffy Duck pajamas, her hair tousled, rubbing her brown eyes. She is healthy, whole. How fortunate I am, how fragile is a Jew's existence.

Even before I lost my father I imagined what it might be like to have my parents die. Now I imagine my child used for target practice, thrown out of a ghetto window, suddenly separated from me at a surprise aktion or during a selection at a railway platform before entering a concentration camp. How would I feel about my own life?

How would it feel to have one's child murdered before one's eyes? It seems insufficient to accept the almost casual adage, life simply goes on. At best, I can only imagine a rage and sadness forever simmering beneath an exterior that would be going through the motions of living. And what would I think of my fellow man who could so brutalize such an innocent, my precious child?

For several months after Rachel's birth, when I heard or read a Holocaust story that brought tears to my eyes, my impulse was to go to Rachel's clown-wallpapered room and hug her, hold her, see her. I needed to be reassured. I wanted to acknowledge how lucky I was. Rachel was further proof of our people's existence. My family had survived. It was not an illusion.

My wife restrains me. Not only do I live in a past significantly different from present reality, but I find myself already imposing this perspective on my daughter. When she refuses to eat her dinner, I muse that a child might have risked her life for that meat and vegetable (or for much less) in the ghetto. Food. Always a startling reminder.

Choices. I think about choices made for our children, both mine and those made by just a generation before me. To which school should I send Rachel? When should she start her toilet training? With how many activities should I involve her?

A mere forty-five years ago, the options were different. Do I send my child to what I hope is a safer place with gentile strangers, perhaps never to see her again? Do I let her go outside the ghetto to forage for food, knowing the punishment incurred if caught? In 1943, my mother, posing as the aunt of a Catholic girl whose mother had already been killed, placed my sister in a convent outside of Warsaw for safekeeping. On one visit to the convent, my mother was told by a nun that a local aristocrat had come to the convent, met her "niece," and was willing to adopt her. How lucky you are, your niece will be safe with him, my mother was told. At that instant my mother decided to tell the Mother Superior the truth and remove her daughter from the safety of the convent if necessary. The Mother Superior's surprised reaction included, "Wouldn't you rather she be able to live a Catholic than face certain death if you take her away?" My mother's reply was, "I would rather her die a Jew than grow up a Catholic."

Children chose as well. During a selection in Auschwitz, an adolescent daughter purposefully preceded her mother in line so that she would not be confronted with the decision of whether or not to follow her mother to a gas chamber.

Survivors grappled with the issue of legacy, with what the children, the second generation, should know about the Holocaust, about the personal perils that their parents endured. Many children of survivors, once removed, face this quandary as well. How steeped do I wish my son or daughter to be in the Holocaust? How should I present the material? At what age should I expose them to which details? The second generation can exert more regulation over the transmission process than did their parents, whose impulses, nightmares, and anger often intruded involuntarily, spasmodically.

Rachel will see the Holocaust books lining my shelves. She will be free to read as much or as little as she chooses. She will know that I write about, speak about, and teach the subject. But how central do I wish this epoch to be in her life? Is this a frame of reference I wish to perpetuate or shield her from? How much of the Holocaust's delayed effects on me will I share with her? I believe it is important to be familiar with those past events. I also know it can be depressing always to carry them in one's mind.

At official gatherings of survivors, speakers routinely invoke one of the rationales for the assemblage and a primary motivating force for more than one survivor's life: we must not let the world forget. Acknowledging the advancing age of the audience, speakers delegate the task of memorializing the six million to the second generation. When one scans the crowd, however, one understands that those hopes are being reposed in a fairly uninhabited vessel. There are few younger individuals in attendance.

To my continual amazement, most second-generation children I encounter have little knowledge of the Holocaust. Many do not want to know. Perhaps they feel too uncomfortable acknowledging their parents' present wounds or past unspoken trauma. Perhaps they fear being dragged downward into a morass of unmentionable horror. Perhaps they simply do not care to be bothered by something that occurred before they were born. Joanne, a child of survivors, remarked: "All I ever knew about my parents' experience was that they met and fell in love in a concentration camp. So I grew up with a very romanticized notion of what occurred during the Holocaust."

Those children actively involved in second-generation organizations, though conscious of their own and their parents' psychological response to the Holocaust, all too often seem to have little interest in learning about the historical, political, and cultural factors that allowed the Nazis to come to power, flourish, and wreak havoc upon the Jewish people. Their "emotional knowledge," they believe, is sufficient.

If those closest to the Holocaust's effects do not wish any involvement, either intellectual or emotional, who can I rely on to perpetuate its memory? I already feel lonely in the battle for remembrance among my contemporaries. Even Jews verbalize being tired of hearing about it.

So I think of Rachel, the third generation. Can I count on her? Can I place that burden upon her? Parents have many common fantasies about their child's developmental milestones. Perhaps it is that first play or recital in which she performs, the first book she reads, the first time she asks you about yourself. I imagine Rachel lighting one of the six symbolic candles at Holocaust commemorations, connecting her to the one million murdered Jewish children.

How to balance my desire for my daughter to know and my hope that she develop as a fearless, undespairing individual? The narrative of the Holocaust must not simply engender a traumatic or vigilant response. I hope it will motivate her to contribute in her own way to the renewed vitality of our people. Being a Jew must be an *affirmative* experience. The potential joys of Judaism, whether they be religious or cultural, must predominate over past and present travails.

More than a third of my sample were parents. Those who did not have offspring or those who had very young children had, for the most part, not given much thought to integrating the history of the Holocaust and its familial consequences into their parenting. They had not considered the extent to which they wished their child to identify himself or herself as a member of the third generation. Parents of older children grappled with their own conflict about imposing a Holocaust legacy. Perhaps they had to assess or clarify the Holocaust's shadow on themselves before they could come to grips with decisions of whether or how to communicate Holocaust-related events. Then, of course, the question remains, At what age should one's child receive selected material?

Although those researchers and clinicians particularly interested in the psychological aftermath of the Holocaust have been asking questions with greater frequency concerning the Holocaust's impact on the third generation, little information is available. Still, from the parenting attitude of the second generation, we may get a glimpse into the future psychological constitution of their children. I asked my respondents, "How has your parents' experience during the Holocaust affected the way you raise your children?"

It is not unusual for children to promise never to repeat the patterns of their parents that brought them pain or hampered their growth. Those in my study, however, emphasized issues specific to their family dynamics. Although not always successful in practice, they wished to allow their children greater freedom and avoid an overly protective or smothering stance that stifles expression and exploration. Many wanted to dispel any fears of the outside world, recoiling from the mistrustful, suspicious attitude their parents transmitted to them. Some vowed to demonstrate greater empathy and provide a more emotionally available parent than their own.

"I want to let her be more independent than my mother was with me. I'll try to stand back more and let her make her own mistakes. . . . We show a lot of affection in our family. I don't know if it's their experience in the Holocaust or the way they raised me, but my parents didn't, although we always knew they cared. All the things we never did as a family because my parents worked so hard and didn't have much money, we now do. We're also more of a family unit. For example, we discuss more things together."

"I do a lot of the same things my parents did with me. I have the 'How could you do this to me after all I've done for you' attitude they had. . . . I have to consciously sit at the opposite side of the table from my daughter who is a poor eater and control myself from pushing food down her throat. . . . Sometimes I blow up, hit the ceiling like my parents did. I have a short fuse."

"I specifically chose a school for my children totally opposite to the yeshiva I grew up in. I try very hard not to replicate what my parents did with me. I don't want my kids to have those fearful, paranoid feelings I always had. . . . I don't give them much religion. I want to give them some identity. I want them to know they are Jewish, but not get depressed by it."

"My daughter is only three but I plan to raise her as I was raised— in a Jewish environment, Hebrew school, Jewish organizations, and so on. However, I want there to be more non-Jews in our home."

"I think I try to be very conscious about not being overly protective. I grit my teeth and let them climb trees, use knives, and so on. I also try to communicate very clearly about feelings and encourage them to do so as well. I try to take their feelings very seriously and treat them with respect."

"Because my parents instilled a great deal of guilt, I'm going to try not to do that. I want them to have a greater breadth of experience, to know that there is a wider world out there. At the same time I want them to know their background and go to Jewish schools. My parents were very clinging—give me a pinch, give me a kiss! They needed affirmation that their children loved them. I think their sense of loss was so great during the Holocaust, they became too overbearing. I'm going to be less overbearing."

Some children of survivors communicated their own insecurities to the third generation as they emphasized their membership in a historically vulnerable minority group. All the participants in this cluster were women. Once again, perhaps this is evidence of a greater fear of persecution among women than men of the second generation. It is not, I believe, that women of the second generation are more likely than their male counterparts to *anticipate* assault. More likely, it is that the men believe they are better equipped to defend themselves against a future onslaught. Be strong, assertive, and vigilant, they teach their offspring. Do not succumb to the role of victim.

> "I teach my children to be able to take care of themselves at an earlier age [than if there had been no Holocaust]. You never know what's going to happen tomorrow. . . . I definitely want to make them aware of the hows and whys of Judaism and not simply cultural Judaism. . . . I want them to understand what anti-Semitism is, to prepare them for anything that might happen, to make them strong people. I want to raise them to be more alert to what people are all about. Jews can't have a simple, normal life. There's so much more that they will need in order to cope."

> "I believe in telling them everything. They need to learn and know. I want them to be able to answer strongly if someone says something anti-Semitic. When Reagan went to Bitburg and the pope went to Austria, I taught them they must speak up."

> "I make sure my children and my parents spend a great deal of time together because I never had grandparents and I want my children to enjoy it. I don't want my children to know the pain of the Holocaust, but I don't want them to simply know about it as history. I want them to feel it, and for it to be a part of their life. . . . It affects a value system I want them to have, for example, being sensitive to the needs of others. . . . I want them to be able to fight for themselves."

A few subjects were aware that their hyperemotionality had already infected their children. Not surprisingly, parental fear and pessimism were driving these excessive reactions.

"I think the only way this [my Holocaust background] has affected my raising my child is in my emotional makeup. I am an easily excitable person with a lot of highs and lows. I tend to get upset about things sometimes when I should remain calm. This has affected the way I reacted to the little aggravations in raising a child, I'm sure; also, the way I overworry about the big issues and problems. . . . I can see that my tensions with [my child] cause him tension in turn—the same pattern as between my parents and myself but not as paranoid."

"I have a terrible fear of authority and a sense of doom. As a result, my children are sensitive to those issues as well. My children are very fearful kids."

Several respondents were intent on instilling a distinctive Jewish pride in their children. Perhaps, because of their experience, they were also determined to emphasize the positive aspects of Jewish identity as opposed to the unsettling, dangerous features their own parents had accentuated. This was Marty's approach. "I'm *very* conscious of giving them a Jewish background, giving them a sense of pride about being Jewish. My eldest is nine and we've just broached the subject. We won't talk about the Holocaust as much in our home as my parents did, but the emphasis on Jewish identity will be even stronger. They go to Hebrew day school and we keep kosher in our home. It's really important for us to make Judaism a positive, happy experience for them."

Becoming a parent often precipitates reflection about our childhood and relationships with our parents. Rachel's presence reminds me of a crucial difference between her childhood world and my own. She will have grandparents. She will, therefore, enjoy more love, more security, more personal contact with her history.

I know of many instances where survivors have spoken in more detail about their prewar life or Holocaust experiences with their grandchildren than with their children. Despite its having become more socially normative for survivors to talk openly of the Holocaust, not having broached the subject for so many years with their own children may make it more difficult for survivors to speak with them now. There are also the emotional encumbrances of their relationships with their own children which may produce obstacles to disclosure. As survivors age, their need to tell of what they have seen and endured becomes more urgent. The third generation, one generation removed from the survivor, provides a more comfortable and, in some cases, more receptive and interested audience. Survivors can relax somewhat, therefore, as they and their stories are assured of continuity.

The flow of generations seems more natural once again. The roots of our family tree are spreading more firmly. Rachel replenishes both my family and her people. And despite Herculean efforts by our enemies throughout the centuries, she is further testimony to their failed attempts to extinguish us.

10

The Legacy

Shema

You who live secure
In your warm houses,
Who, returning at evening, find
Hot food and friendly faces:
 Consider whether this is a man,
 Who labours in the mud
 Who knows no peace
 Who fights for a crust of bread
 Who dies at a yes or a no.
 Consider whether this is a woman,
 Without hair or name
 With no more strength to remember
 Eyes empty and womb cold
 As a frog in winter.
Consider that this has been:
I commend these words to you.
Engrave them on your hearts
When you are in your house, when you walk on your way
When you go to bed, when you rise:
Repeat them to your children.
 Or may your house crumble,
 Disease render you powerless,
 Your offspring avert their faces from you.

         —Primo Levi
         January 10, 1946

Survivors don't have a choice. Children of survivors do. For survivors, memory is involuntary. It brutally intrudes during their morning coffee, during their afternoon grocery shopping. It pierces their sleep, causing them to awaken as if stabbed by a familiar, terrifying intruder. The past commingles with the present. Always.

Many survivors were reluctant to burden their children with the Holocaust. They refrained from talking about what they saw, heard, felt, endured. Others selectively informed their children, some from the beginning, some only recently. These survivors implored their children to remember. But, to what end? To know what life was like before the war, what life could have been like if it had not happened? To know what had been so violently wrested from them? Did these survivors simply crave a fuller understanding of them by others? Did they perhaps want their children to be aware of the outer limits of man's cruelty, so they could be prepared?

Those in the second generation have more voluntary control. They can choose to ask more, read more, think more about the Holocaust. And, if they decide to immerse themselves in that era, they will be confronted with determinations. How much will I live in the past as opposed to the present? To what extent will I allow past events to affect my expectations for the future?

For many children of survivors, connections have not yet been made. In Los Angeles, there has been, for the past four years, an annual picnic and fair, organized by second-generation members for the survivor community. One year I noticed a stranger walking around the grounds rather aimlessly. He suddenly stopped, sat on the grass, buried his head in his hands, and sobbed. Later, in conversation, he disclosed that he had avoided anything to do with the Holocaust and survivors his entire adult life. Walking among the accents, the numbers, the tatoos, he understood that this was his place. Many of those I questioned in the course of this study acknowledged that the interview was the first time they had ever inspected their relationship to the Holocaust.

Only by learning about the past can we have some appreciation of what was lost, destroyed. And, perhaps, only through knowledge of the Holocaust and our parents can those in the second generation fully understand themselves.

Remembering may necessitate mourning. Some survivors have continuing elevated levels of anger, depression, and guilt, partially as a result of their inability or unwillingness to grieve fully for their loss of family members, a perceived idyllic life, and aspects of themselves either discarded or violently stolen. Many children of survivors also feel anger and depression because of Holocaust-related deprivations (grandparents, for example, or a more emotionally available parent). They, too, have skirted the mourning process. Their difficulty in fully and appropriately mourning, however, is understandable, as the objects of loss are less tangible. As one child of survivors has written: "Yet, the empty imprint of those lost relatives ironically serves to heighten a sense of family. It is imagining a world without the aid of one picture or memento, while devouring collective histories and political events of the preceding several decades as though the absorption of a mass of anonymous documents would yield a composite picture of a family past."[1]

There are public commemorations with speeches, candle-lighting ceremonies, first-person accounts, dramatic readings, and prayers for the dead. The Six Day War of 1967 focused greater attention on the observance of Yom Hashoah (Holocaust Day), the day on which the six million dead are memorialized; it is now observed on the twenty-seventh day of the Hebrew month of Nisan in Jewish communities around the world. The Six Day War conjured up associations with the annihilation of the recent past. On this occasion, however, the outcome was deliverance instead of destruction, and the Israeli victory renewed a pride in Jewish identity.

Seven years ago, during a break in one of my lectures in a course on psychopathology, I overheard a fragment of a conversation between two undergraduate students.

"My parents went through the Holocaust in Europe."
"Yeah, my parents probably had it just as tough. They went through the depression in the United States."

It was at that moment I decided I must teach about the Holocaust.

We remember so that we can teach. We carry on tradition, speak the Yiddish language of our grandparents so that something of them continues. But perhaps those of the second generation must find their own way to commemorate and not simply follow the lead of their parents. The experience of the Holocaust by the child is obviously a different one from that of the survivor. And, out of that different experience, a different response must come.

Children of survivors vary tremendously in their involuntary or volitional emotional closeness to the Holocaust. Some have embraced their calamitous background, others have fled the potential dread. Those siblings raised in the same home often diverge in their historical interest, feelings about the parenting they received, perception of the gentile world, attitudes toward intermarriage, and so on. As mentioned earlier, it has been suggested that firstborn children absorbed the brunt of parental insecurities born of the proximity to the Holocaust and the newly adopted status of immigrant. Regarding this generalization and many others generated by previous investigators, I found numerous exceptions in my sample. One must never underestimate the role of the genetic temperament in any individual's reaction to his or her environment.

Those in the second generation (who have not already done so) might benefit from a closer examination of their relationships with their survivor parents. Many children describe intense but superficial ties. Survivors have often been reluctant to relate their experiences, for fear of harming their children or of confronting aspects of their own past. Some children of survivors maintain a certain distance in order to avoid being engulfed by their parents. Oftentimes, they are also motivated by a desire to protect themselves or their parents from further disappointment.

Greater communication, I believe, by parents about their past experiences and the continuing effects of those experiences (assuming, of course, that they are not simply trying to make their children feel guilty or to control them) usually not only produces greater intimacy between parents and children but also provides a greater recognition of the strength of the survivors. As a result, children may view their parents with more respect and at the same time feel freer to admit their own difficulties without fear of causing unmanageable distress to their mothers or fathers. Many children of survivors have asserted that their reluctance to broach the subject of a parent's past travails comes from their desire to refrain from stirring painful memories and shaking a perceived fragile adaptation. This rationalization often reflects a projection of the child's fears. Indeed, the child may wish to avoid the subject because of his or her own anxieties that are generated by the recounting of those events.

At the junction of their identity as a Jew and as a child of survivors, many in the second generation have nourished a self-image of victim. They feel victimized by the Nazis who denied them an extended family and disabled their parents. They may also feel victimized by parents who denied them the untainted, more "normal" atmosphere they observed in the homes of their American peers. The children of survivors, therefore, must consciously provide a counterweight to this part of their Jewish identity (that is, the victim), which brings despair and anger, by living and attending to the richness and beauty of their heritage as well.

Where and how one chooses to focus one's attention will affect one's self-image. What are the consequences of defining oneself primarily as a victim? Moreover, what happens if one aggravates that picture by illuminating a yellow Star of David covering one's heart? For example, modern Jewish liberal tradition has been distinguished by its identification with and support for the oppressed. Children of survivors, on the other hand, although they commonly acknowledge psychological problems and a strong Jewish identity as direct results of their parents' Holocaust experience, do not necessarily evidence a great tolerance for other minorities. Those found to be the most tolerant of other minority groups were those children of survivors with the greatest historical knowledge of the Holocaust.[2] An exclusive emotional response by those of the second generation is insufficient. Greater erudition and resulting cognitive understanding are necessary if we are to move beyond an exclusive, parochial focus.

In conclusion, one might ask, What is the second generation's responsibility to their ancestors? In 1980, at the first international gathering of Holocaust survivors that took place in Jerusalem, the children proclaimed, "We accept the legacy of the Holocaust." That legacy must not simply be confined to keeping the memory of the Holocaust alive and undistorted. It must include an enrichment of the Jewish people whose resources were so depleted in recent times. That task is especially difficult of course because the zeitgeist of the prewar eastern European Jewish community with its suffusion of Jewish culture has been destroyed. Then, one did not have to exert oneself in order to learn about and contribute to the vibrancy of one's people. We, in the postwar generation, however, must employ a much greater effort.

Appendix

The Questionnaire
Used in My Study

Age: Sex:

Place of birth:

How many siblings do you have?

What is your position relative to your siblings (oldest, youngest, middle)?

Occupation:

Marital status (check one):

  Single   Married   Divorced   Widowed

Do you have any children?   if yes, how many?

Did you go to synagogue last Yom Kippur?

Have you ever been in psychotherapy?   If yes, for how long?

Approximately how many non-holiday Sabbaths a year do you attend synagogue?

When did your parents leave Europe? Father: Mother:

In which city do you live?

Are one or both of your parents Holocaust survivors?
If only one, which one?

How much do you know about your parents' experiences during the Holocaust? How did you find out? How old were you when you learned of them?

How do you believe your parents' experiences during the Holocaust affected the way they raised you as a child?

How has your family's Holocaust background affected your attitude toward non-Jews?

How do you feel about being Jewish?

(Only answer the following question if you have children.)
How has your parents' experience during the Holocaust affected the way you raise your children?

Would you marry a non-Jew? Why or why not? If you are already married, would you have considered marrying a non-Jew while you were single? Please explain your answer.

How has the Holocaust affected your outlook on life?

Have you ever had psychological problems which you would at least partially attribute to your family's Holocaust background? Please explain what those problems are.

Do you have any particular psychological strengths which you would at least partially attribute to your family's Holocaust background? Please explain what those strengths are.

Do you ever have dreams which are Holocaust related? If so, please describe the dreams in as much detail as possible.

Do you believe there could be another attempted Jewish Holocaust? Please explain your answer.

Please describe any Holocaust-related activities (e.g., groups, educational programs) in which you are presently involved.

In what ways (if any) do you perceive your survivor parent(s) to be abnormal as a result of their experience?

Do you believe your parents related to you any differently than non-survivor Jewish parents relate to their children? Please explain your answer.

How has the Holocaust affected your belief in God?

How would you describe your parents' marital relationship? Please describe it as completely as possible.

Have you ever been to Israel? If so, how many times? Please explain your psychological/emotional relationship to Israel.

Do you have more Jewish close friends than non-Jewish close friends? Is this at all related to the Holocaust?

Notes

Chapter 1. The Psychological Profile of Survivors

1. William C. Niederland, "Psychiatric Disorders among Persecution Victims: A Contribution to the Understanding of Concentration Camp Pathology and Its Aftereffects," *Journal of Nervous and Mental Diseases* 139 (1964): 458–74.

2. Leo Eitinger, *Concentration Camp Survivors in Norway and Israel* (London: Allen and Unwin, 1964), 190.

3. Robert J. Lifton, "Witnessing Survival," *Transactions* (Mar. 1978): 40–44.

4. Henry Krystal, "Patterns of Psychological Damage," in *Massive Psychic Trauma*, ed. Henry Krystal (New York: International Universities Press, 1968).

5. Robert J. Lifton, "Survivors of Hiroshima and Nazi Persecution," in Krystal, *Massive Psychic Trauma*.

6. Robert J. Lifton, *Death in Life: Survivors of Hiroshima* (New York: Random House, 1976); Lifton, *The Broken Connection: On Death and the Continuity of Life* (New York: Basic Books, 1979).

7. Krystal, *Massive Psychic Trauma*, 4.

8. Primo Levi, *The Drowned and the Saved* (New York: Summit, 1988), 76, 78.

9. Lifton, "Survivors of Hiroshima," 179.

10. Levi, *The Drowned and the Saved*, 81.

11. Ibid., 75.

12. Lisa Newman, "Emotional Disturbances in Children of Holocaust Survivors," *Social Casework: The Journal of Contemporary Social Work* 60 (Jan. 1979): 43–50.

13. Dov Aleksandrowicz, "Children of Concentration Camp Survivors," *Yearbook of the International Association for Child Psychiatry and Allied Professions*, vol. 2 (New York: John Wiley, 1973), 383–94.

14. J. Elzas, "Assistance Scheme for Victims of Persecution 1940–1945: Statistics on Applicants for Assistance" (Submitted proposal to Netherlands Information Office, Jerusalem, 1988); J. Izaks, "Effects of the Holocaust on Dutch Jewish Victims, Residents of Israel: Thirty Years Afterward" (Master's thesis, Bar-Ilan University, 1984); Haim

Dasberg and R. Kaufman, "ELAH: A Unique Psychosocial Mental Health Organization for Dutch Holocaust Survivors in Israel" (Paper delivered at the International Conference on the Holocaust and Genocide, Tel-Aviv, 1982); and M. Cohen, "An Inquiry on Needs for Psychosocial Help to Dutch Victims of World War II Living in Israel" (Proposal submitted to ELAH Foundation, Ramat Gan, 1986).

15. Krystal, *Massive Psychic Trauma*, 1–8.

16. I. Levav and J. Abramson, "Emotional Distress among Concentration Camp Survivors: A Community Study in Jerusalem," *Psychological Medicine* 14 (1984): 215–18; D. Carmil and R. Carel, "Emotional Distress and Satisfaction in Life among Holocaust Survivors: A Community Study of Survivors and Controls," *Psychological Medicine* 16 (1986): 141–49.

17. W. Eaton et al., "Impairment in Holocaust Survivors after Thirty-three Years: Data from an Unbiased Community Sample," *American Journal of Psychiatry* 139 (1982): 773–77.

18. Lifton, "Witnessing Survival," 40–44.

19. Martin Bergmann and Milton Jacovy, eds., *Generations of the Holocaust* (New York: Basic Books, 1982), 4–32.

20. Paul Chodoff, "Effects of Extreme Coercive and Oppressive Forces," in *American Handbook of Psychiatry*, ed. Silvano Arieti (New York: Basic Books, 1959); Kurt Eissler, "Perverted Psychiatry?" *American Journal of Psychiatry* 123 (1968): 1352–58.

21. Hillel Klein, "Child of Holocaust: Mourning and Bereavement," in *The Child in His Family*, vol. 2, ed. E. James Anthony (New York: Wiley, 1973), 393–409.

22. William C. Niederland, "An Interpretation of the Psychological Stresses and Defenses in Concentration Camp Life and the Late Aftereffects," in Krystal, *Massive Psychic Trauma*, 63.

23. Krystal, *Massive Psychic Trauma*, 3.

24. Aaron Antonowsky et al., "Twenty-five Years Later: A Limited Study of Sequelae of the Concentration Camp Experience," *Social Psychiatry* 6 (1971): 186–93; Jackie Lomranz et al., "Time Orientation in Nazi Concentration Camp Survivors: Forty Years After," *American Journal of Orthopsychiatry* 55 (1985): 230–36.

25. Bruno Bettelheim, *The Informed Heart* (New York: Free Press, 1960).

26. Bruno Bettelheim, *Surviving and Other Essays* (New York: Knopf, 1979).

27. Levi, *The Drowned and the Saved*, 47.

28. Yael Danieli, "The Treatment and Prevention of Long-Term Effects and Intergenerational Transmission of Victimization: A Lesson from Holocaust Survivors and Their Children," in *Trauma and Its Wake*, ed. C. Figley (New York: Brunner/Mazel, 1985), 295–313.

29. Krystal, *Massive Psychic Trauma*, 190.

30. Leo Eitinger, "Cross Cultural Perspective on Children of Survivors" (Panel presentation at the First International Conference on Children of Holocaust Survivors, New York, 1979).

31. Yael Danieli, "On the Achievement of Integration in Aging Survivors of the Nazi Holocaust," *Journal of Geriatric Psychiatry* 14 (1981): 191–210.

32. Robert Krell, "Child Survivors of the Holocaust: Forty Years Later," *Journal of the American Academy of Child Psychiatry* 24 (1985): 377–412.

Chapter 2. Intergenerational Transmission

1. Judith Kestenberg, "Psychoanalytic Contributions to the Problem of Survivors from Nazi Persecution," *Israel Annals of Psychiatry and Related Disciplines* 10 (1972): 311–

25; Bernard Trossman, "Adolescent Children of Concentration Camp Survivors," *Canadian Psychiatric Association Journal* 12 (1968): 121–23.

2. Harvey Barocas and Carol Barocas, "Manifestations of Concentration Camp Effects on the Second Generation," *American Journal of Psychiatry* 130 (1973): 820–21.

3. Anna Kolodner, "The Socialization of Children of Concentration Camp Survivors" (Ph.D. diss., Boston University, 1987).

4. Barocas and Barocas, "Concentration Camp Effects," 821.

5. Axel Russell, "Late Psychosocial Consequences in Concentration Camp Survivor Families," *American Journal of Orthopsychiatry* 44 (1974): 611–19.

6. Robert Prince, "Second Generation Effects of Historical Trauma," *Psychoanalytic Review* 72 (1985): 9–29.

7. Stephen Sonnenberg, "Workshop Report: Children of Survivors," *Journal of the American Psychoanalytic Association* 22 (1974): 200–204.

8. Cipora Katz and Franklin Keleman, "The Children of Holocaust Survivors: Issues of Separation," *Journal of Jewish Communal Service* 57 (1981): 257–63.

9. Ibid., 262.

10. Hillel Klein, "Families of Holocaust Survivors in the Kibbutz: Psychological Studies," in *Psychic Traumatization,* ed. Henry Krystal and William C. Niederland (Boston: Little, Brown, 1971), 67–92; Vivian Rakoff, "Long Term Effects of the Concentration Camp," *Viewpoint,* March 1966, 17–21; Barocas and Barocas, "Concentration Camp Effects," 821.

11. Axel Russell et al., "Adaptive Abilities in Non-Clinical Second Generation Holocaust Survivors and Controls: A Comparison," *American Journal of Psychotherapy* 39 (1985): 564–79.

12. Katz and Keleman, "Children of Holocaust Survivors," 257–63.

13. M. Bergmann and M. Jacovy, eds., *Generations of the Holocaust* (New York: Basic Books, 1982), 101.

14. Theo DeGraff, "Pathological Patterns of Identification in Families of Survivors of the Holocaust," *Israel Annals of Psychiatry and Related Disciplines* 13 (1975): 335–63; L. Rosenberger, "Children of Survivors," in *The Child in His Family,* vol. 2, ed. E. James Anthony and Cyrille Koupernik (New York: Wiley, 1974), 375–77.

15. Marvin Lipkowitz, "The Child of Two Survivors," *Israel Annals of Psychiatry and Related Disciplines* 11 (1973): 141–55; Sonnenberg, "Workshop Report," 200–204.

16. Marion Oliner, in Bergmann and Jacovy, *Generations of the Holocaust,* 267.

17. Trossman, "Children of Survivors," 121–23.

18. Prince, "Effects of Historical Trauma," 9–29.

19. Katz and Keleman, "Children of Holocaust Survivors," 257–63.

20. Russell, "Psychosocial Consequences in Survivor Families," 611–19.

21. Klein, "Families of Survivors in the Kibbutz," 83.

22. John Sigal and Vivian Rakoff, "Concentration Camp Survival: A Pilot Study of Effects on the Second Generation," *Canadian Psychiatric Association Journal* 16 (1971): 393–97.

23. Harvey Barocas, "Children of Purgatory: Reflections on the Concentration Camp Survival Syndrome," *Corrective Psychiatry and Journal of Social Therapy* 16 (1970): 51–58.

24. H. Barocas, "Manifestations of Concentration Camp Effects on the Second Generation," *International Journal of Social Psychiatry* 21 (1975): 88.

25. Trossman, "Children of Survivors," 121–23; Kolodner, "Children of Concentration Camp Survivors."

26. Barocas and Barocas, "Concentration Camp Effects," 821.

27. Trossman, "Children of Survivors," 121–23.

28. Prince, "Effects of Historical Trauma," 9–29.

29. Shamai Davidson, "Transgenerational Transmission in the Families of Holocaust Survivors," *International Journal of Family Psychiatry* 1 (1980): 95–112.

30. Prince, "Effects of Historical Trauma," 9–29.

31. Helen Epstein, *Children of the Holocaust* (New York: Putnam, 1979), 1.

32. Deborah Berger, "Children of Nazi Holocaust Survivors: A Coming of Age" (Master's thesis, Goddard College, 1980), 5.

33. DeGraff, "Patterns of Identification," 335–63.

34. Norman Solkoff, "Children of Survivors of the Nazi Holocaust: A Critical Review of the Literature," *American Journal of Orthopsychiatry* 51 (1981): 29–42.

35. Kolodner, "Children of Concentration Camp Survivors," 22.

36. H. Goldkorn-Lichtman, "Children of Survivors of the Nazi Holocaust: A Personality Study" (Ph.D. diss., Jerusalem, 1983).

37. Jeffrey Goodman, "The Transmission of Parental Trauma: Second Generation Effects of Nazi Concentration Camp Survival" (Ph.D. diss., California School of Professional Psychology, Fresno, 1978).

38. Stephen Karr, "Second Generation Effects of the Nazi Holocaust" (Ph.D. diss., California School of Professional Psychology, San Francisco, 1973).

39. Norman Blumenthal, "Factors Contributing to Varying Levels of Adjustment among Children of Holocaust Survivors," *Dissertation Abstracts International* 42 (1981): 1596B.

40. Zoli Zlotogorski, "Offspring of Concentration Camp Survivors: The Relationship of Perceptions of Family Cohesion and Adaptability to Levels of Ego Functioning," *Dissertation Abstracts International* 42 (1982): 3452B.

41. John Sigal, "Second Generation Effects of Massive Psychic Trauma," in Krystal and Niederland, *Psychic Traumatization*, 55–65.

42. United States: G. Leon et al., "Survivors of the Holocaust and Their Children: Current Status and Adjustment," *Journal of Personality and Social Psychology* 41 (1981): 503–18. Israel: Dov Aleksandrowicz, "Children of Concentration Camp Survivors," in *The Child in His Family*, 385–92; Miriam Gay and Jonah Fuchs, "Characteristics of the Offspring of Holocaust Survivors in Israel," *Mental Health and Society* 1 (1974): 302–14; Uriel Last and Hillel Klein, "The Transgenerational Impact" (Manuscript, Jerusalem, 1980); Miriam Gay and S. Shulman, "Comparison of Children of Holocaust Survivors with Children of the General Population in Israel" (Manuscript, Jerusalem, 1980).

43. Vivian Rakoff et al., "Children of Families of Concentration Camp Survivors," *Canada's Mental Health* 14 (1966): 24–26; Trossman, "Children of Survivors," 121–23; John Sigal et al., "Some Second Generation Effects of Surviving the Nazi Persecution," *American Journal of Orthopsychiatry* 43 (1973): 320–28.

44. Stephen Karr, "The Children of the Holocaust: A Study in the Transmission of Trauma" (Paper presented at the Research Conference, Mount Zion Hospital and Medical Center, San Francisco, 1977).

45. Prince, "Effects of Historical Trauma," 27.

46. Shamai Davidson, "Transgenerational Transmission in the Families of Holocaust Survivors," *International Journal of Family Psychiatry* 1 (1980): 98.

47. Florabel Kinsler, "Second Generation Effects of the Holocaust: The Effectiveness of Group Therapy in the Resolution of the Transmission of Parental Trauma," *Journal of Psychology and Judaism* 6 (1981): 53–67; Martin Bergmann, "Thoughts on Superego Pathology of Survivors and Their Children," in Bergmann and Jacovy, *Generations of the Holocaust*, 287–309.

48. Lawrence Hanover, "Parent-Child Relationships of Survivors of the Nazi Holocaust," *Dissertation Abstracts International* 42 (1981): 770B.

49. Russell et al., "Adaptive Abilities in the Second Generation," 564–79.

50. Prince, "Effects of Historical Trauma," 19.
51. Karr, "The Transmission of Trauma," 11–12.

Chapter 3. "For this I survived the camps?"

1. Lawrence Hanover, "Parent-Child Relationships of Survivors of the Nazi Holocaust," *Dissertation Abstracts International*, 42 (1981): 770B. Sarah Shiryon, "The Second Generation Leaves Home: The Function of the Sibling Subgroup in the Separation-Individuation Process of the Survivor Family" (Paper presented at the International Conference on the Holocaust and Genocide, Tel-Aviv, 1982).

2. Harvey Barocas and Carol Barocas, "Separation-Individuation Conflicts in Children of Holocaust Survivors," *Journal of Contemporary Psychotherapy* 11 (1980): 6–14.

3. Axel Russell, "Late Psychosocial Consequences in Concentration Camp Survivor Families," *American Journal of Orthopsychiatry* 44 (1974): 611–19; John Sigal and Vivian Rakoff, "Concentration Camp Survival: A Pilot Study of the Effects on the Second Generation," *Journal of the Canadian Psychiatric Association* 16 (1971): 390–93; John Sigal, "Second Generation Effects of Massive Psychic Trauma," in *Psychic Traumatization*, ed. Henry Krystal and William C. Niederland (Boston: Little, Brown, 1971).

4. Bernard Trossman, "Adolescent Children of Concentration Camp Survivors," *Canadian Psychiatric Association Journal* 12 (1968): 121–23.

5. Robert Krell, "Holocaust Families: The Survivors and Their Children," *Comprehensive Psychiatry* 20 (1979): 564.

6. H. Lichtman, "Parental Communication of Holocaust Experiences and Personality Characteristics among Second Generation Survivors," *Journal of Clinical Psychology* 40 (1984): 914–24.

7. L. Rosenberger, "Children of Survivors," in *The Child in His Family*, ed. E. Anthony and C. Koupernik (New York: Wiley, 1974).

8. Anna Kolodner, "The Socialization of Children of Concentration Camp Survivors" (Ph.D. diss., Boston University, 1987).

9. Lenore Podietz et al., "Engagement in Families of Holocaust Survivors," *Journal of Marital and Family Therapy* 10 (1984): 49.

10. John Sigal et al., "Some Second Generation Effects of Surviving the Nazi Persecution," *American Journal of Orthopsychiatry* 43 (1973): 320–28; Podietz et al., "Engagement in Families of Holocaust Survivors," 43–51.

11. John Sigal and Vivian Rakoff, "Concentration Camp Survival: A Pilot Study of Effects on the Second Generation," *Canadian Psychiatric Association Journal* 16 (1971): 390–93; S. Wolfe, "Researcher Disputes Studies on Children of Survivors," *Northern California Jewish Bulletin*, 11 July 1986.

12. Hillel Klein, "Families of Holocaust Survivors in the Kibbutz: Psychological Studies," in Krystal and Niederland, *Psychic Traumatization*.

13. Sigal and Rakoff, "Effects on the Second Generation," 390–93; Vivian Rakoff et al., "Children of Families of Concentration Camp Survivors," *Canada's Mental Health* 14 (1966): 24–26.

14. Krell, "Holocaust Families," 560–67.

15. Harvey Barocas and Carol Barocas, "Manifestations of Concentration Camp Effects on the Second Generation," *American Journal of Psychiatry* 130 (1973): 820–21.

16. Yael Danieli, "Families of Survivors of the Nazi Holocaust: Some Short and Long Term Effects," in *Psychological Stress and Adjustment in Time of War and Peace*, ed. N. Milgran (Washington: Hemisphere, 1980).

Chapter 4. Recounting the Stories

1. Stephen Karr, "The Children of the Holocaust: A Study in the Transmission of Trauma" (Paper presented at the Research Conference, Mount Zion Hospital and Medical Center, San Francisco, 1977).

2. Martin Bergmann and Milton Jacovy, eds., *Generations of the Holocaust* (New York: Basic Books, 1982), 59.

3. Primo Levi, *The Drowned and the Saved* (New York: Summit, 1988), 12.

4. Ibid., 36.

5. Yael Danieli, "Families of Survivors of the Nazi Holocaust: Some Short and Long Term Effects," in *Psychological Stress and Adjustment in Time of War and Peace*, ed. N. Milgran (Washington: Hemisphere, 1980).

6. Robert Krell, "Holocaust Families: The Survivors and Their Children," *Comprehensive Psychiatry* 20 (1979): 560–67.

7. Hillel Klein, "Holocaust Survivors in Kibbutzim: Readaptation and Reintegration," *Israel Annals of Psychiatry and Related Disciplines* 10 (1972): 78–91.

8. Bernard Trossman, "Adolescent Children of Concentration Camp Survivors," *Canadian Psychiatric Association Journal* 12 (1968): 121–23.

9. Robert Prince, *The Legacy of the Holocaust: Psychohistorical Themes in the Second Generation* (Ann Arbor: UMI Research Press, 1985).

10. H. Lichtman, "Parental Communication of Holocaust Experiences and Personality Characteristics among Second Generation Survivors," *Journal of Clinical Psychology* 40 (1984): 914–24.

11. Sophie Kav-Venaki and Arie Nadler, "Transgenerational Effects of Massive Psychic Traumatization: Psychological Characteristics of Children of Holocaust Survivors in Israel" (Paper presented at a meeting of the International Society of Political Psychology, Mannheim, 1981).

12. Hillel Klein, "Children of the Holocaust: Mourning and Bereavement," *International Yearbook of the Association for Child Psychiatry and Allied Professions*, vol. 2 (New York: John Wiley, 1973), 393–410.

13. Bergmann and Jacovy, *Generations of the Holocaust*, 311.

14. Prince, *The Legacy of the Holocaust*; Shamai Davidson, "Transgenerational Transmission in the Families of Holocaust Survivors," *International Journal of Family Psychiatry* 1 (1980): 95–112.

15. Danieli, "Families of Survivors."

16. David Heller, "Themes of Culture and Ancestry among Children of Concentration Camp Survivors," *Psychiatry* 45 (1982): 247–61.

Chapter 5. Children Describe Their Parents

1. Robert Prince, *The Legacy of the Holocaust: Psychohistorical Themes in the Second Generation* (Ann Arbor: UMI Research Press, 1985).

2. Lenore Podietz et al., "Engagement in Families of Holocaust Survivors," *Journal of Marital and Family Therapy* 10 (1984): 43–51.

3. Ibid.

4. Uriel Last and Hillel Klein, *The Nazi Concentration Camps* (Jerusalem: Yad Vashem, 1984).

5. Prince, *Legacy of the Holocaust*.

6. Fran Klein-Parker, "Dominant Attitudes of Adult Children of Holocaust Survivors towards Their Parents" (Ph.D. diss., Saybrook Institute, Mich., 1984).

7. Eva Fogelman and Bella Savran, "Therapeutic Groups for Children of Holocaust Survivors," *International Journal of Group Psychotherapy* 29 (1979): 211–36.

8. Quoted in Klein-Parker, "Attitudes of Adult Children of Survivors," 9.

9. Dov Aleksandrowicz, "Children of Concentration Camp Survivors," *Yearbook of the International Association for Child Psychiatry and Allied Professions*, vol. 2 (New York: John Wiley, 1973), 383–94.

10. Last and Klein, *Nazi Concentration Camps*.

11. Miriam Scharf, conversation with author, Dec. 1987.

Chapter 6. Jews and Gentiles

1. Bernard Trossman, "Adolescent Children of Concentration Camp Survivors," *Canadian Psychiatric Journal* 12 (1968): 121–23.

2. Robert Prince, "Second Generation Effects of Historical Trauma," *Psychoanalytic Review* 72 (1985): 9–29.

3. Axel Russell et al., "Adaptive Abilities in Non-Clinical Second Generation Holocaust Survivors and Controls: A Comparison," *American Journal of Psychotherapy* 39 (1985): 564–79.

4. David Heller, "Themes of Culture and Ancestry among Children of Concentration Camp Survivors," *Psychiatry* 45 (1982): 255.

5. B. Weisman, "Acculturation Patterns in Holocaust Survivors and Children of Holocaust Survivors" (Ph.D. diss., California School of Professional Psychology, Los Angeles, 1986).

6. Axel Russell, "Late Psychological Consequences in Concentration Camp Survivor Families," *American Journal of Orthopsychiatry* 44 (1974): 611–19.

7. I. Tauber, "Second Generation Effects of the Nazi Holocaust: A Psychosocial Study of a Non-Clinical Sample in North America" (Ph.D. diss., California School of Professional Psychology, Berkeley, 1980).

8. Marilyn Ludzki, "Children of Survivors," *Jewish Spectator* 42 (1977): 41–43.

9. Cipora Katz and Franklin Keleman, "The Children of Holocaust Survivors: Issues of Separation," *Journal of Jewish Communal Service* 57 (1981): 257–63.

10. Anne Roiphe, *A Season for Healing* (New York: Summit Books, 1988).

Chapter 7. In Case It Should Happen Again

1. Fran Klein-Parker, "Dominant Attitudes of Adult Children of Holocaust Survivors towards Their Parents" (Ph.D. diss., Saybrook Institute, Mich., 1984), 124–26.

2. Ibid., 124.

3. Harvey Barocas and Carol Barocas, "Wounds of the Fathers: The Next Generation of Holocaust Victims," *International Review of Psychoanalysis* 6 (1979): 331–41.

4. Helen Epstein, "The Heirs of the Holocaust," *New York Times Magazine*, 19 June 1977, 14.

Chapter 8. Can I Believe in God?

1. Irving Rosenbaum, *The Holocaust and Halakhah* (New York: Ktav, 1976), 24.

2. Robert Krell, "Holocaust Families: The Survivors and Their Children," *Comprehensive Psychiatry* 20 (1979): 564.

3. Anne Roiphe, *A Season for Healing* (New York: Summit Books, 1988), 56.

4. Krell, "Holocaust Families," 565.

5. Rabbi Yaakov Perlow, in *A Path through the Ashes* (New York: Art Scroll Series, 1986), 76–77, and Rabbi Avrohom Wolf, in *A Path through the Ashes*, 37.

6. E. Wasserman, *Ma'amar Ikvossoh Demeschicho Vema'amar al Ha'emunah. A Belaychtung fun der yetztiger Tekufa* (New York: n.p., 1939).

7. Eliezer Berkovits, *Faith after the Holocaust* (New York: Ktav, 1973), 94.

8. See Berkovits, *Faith after the Holocaust*; Martin Buber, *Eclipse of God* (New York: Harper, 1952); A. Besdin, *Reflections of the Rav* (Jerusalem: Department for Torah Education, 1979), 37.

9. Berkovits, *Faith after the Holocaust*, 106.

Chapter 9. The Third Generation

1. Sarah Nomberg-Przytyk, *Auschwitz: True Tales from a Grotesque Land* (Chapel Hill: University of North Carolina Press, 1985), 70.

Chapter 10. The Legacy

1. H. Wirth-Nesher, "A Dual Legacy: How Is the Child of Holocaust Survivors Different from Other Children?" *Moment*, April 1981, 28.

2. M. Weinfeld and J. Sigal, "The Effect of the Holocaust on Selected Socio-Political Attitudes of Adult Children of Survivors," *Canadian Review of Sociology and Anthropology* 23 (1986): 365–82.

Index of Names

Library of Congress Cataloging-in-Publication Data

Hass, Aaron.
   In the shadow of the Holocaust : the second generation / Aaron
Hass.
      p.   cm.
   Includes bibliographical references.
   Includes index.
   ISBN 0-8014-2477-1 (alk. paper)
      1. Children of Holocaust survivors—United States—Psychology.
   2. Children of Holocaust survivors—United States—Interviews.
   I. Title.
   D804.3.H374   1990
   940.53'18'019—dc20   90-55124